It's like wearing poetry

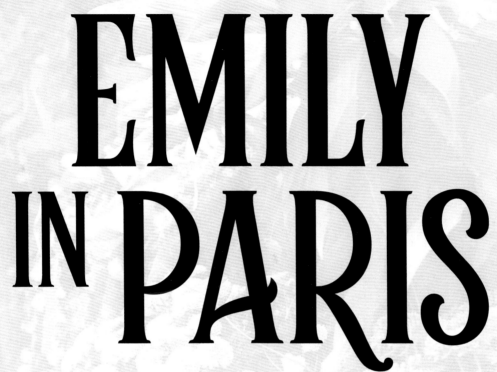

EMILY IN PARIS

The Official Cookbook

Kim Laidlaw

Roses 5,61

weldon**owen**

CONTENTS

LA PÂTISSERIE

LE CAFÉ

LES BASES

Introduction

Few places are more iconic—or drop-dead gorgeous—than Paris, an unforgettable city that epitomizes sophistication and *joie de vivre*. So when Emily Cooper, a young, up-and-coming social media strategist from Chicago, gets the opportunity of a lifetime—to live and work (and eat) in Paris—she jumps at the chance. Through the eyes of Emily, viewers satisfy their wanderlust, following her along the scenic streets of Paris as she buys a pain au chocolat at La Boulangerie Moderne, enjoys a warm crêpe from a takeaway stand (while strolling with a hot guy), sips (plenty of) wine with her friend Mindy at an alfresco table midday, and stops for coffee in stylish cafés.

Her fans sympathize (and cringe) when Emily struggles to understand the norms of French culture and mangles the language, and they cheer when she makes a breakthrough. Her complicated relationships—whether romantic, alluring, strategic, or even antagonistic—often lead to inventive cocktails and hors d'oeuvres at parties and memorable meals at bistros, brasseries, and Gabriel's small, charming restaurant.

Based on the best that France has to offer, this cookbook is filled with the legendary dishes of Paris, Provence, and beyond, highlighting Emily's gastronomic experiences, adventures, and calamities. Salade frisée aux lardons (page 20) and soupe au pistou (page 21) are standard fare in small neighborhood bistros where Emily meets coworkers for a gossipy lunch. Seafood platters (page 63), sole meunière (page 68), and choucroute alsacienne (page 72) are classic options found at the late-night brasseries she frequents. And steak au poivre (page 119) is just the thing to get a cute chef to notice you when you try to send it back at his restaurant. A croissant (page 143) from the local patisserie is the perfect morning treat, a baguette (page 156) with cheese from an outdoor market is just right for a park-bench snack, and what would a late-afternoon trip to a café be without an Aperol spritz (page 179) or a French 75 (page 184)?

Wherever you live, you can experience the marvels of French cuisine through the recipes in these pages, which include everything from cocktails, hors d'oeuvres, salads, and soups to main dishes and desserts. So sit back, relax, and get ready to travel through Emily's Paris!

Darren Star,
Creator and Executive Producer, *Emily in Paris*

UN
LE BISTRO

Artichokes with Aioli

Steamed, braised, or grilled, artichokes appear on restaurant and home dinner tables throughout France. In Provence, they are often served with aioli, the region's popular garlic-kissed mayonnaise. Look for green globe artichokes or the smaller, pretty purple-tinged variety that is common in southern France.

makes 4 servings

AIOLI

2 cloves garlic

¼ teaspoon fine sea salt

1 cup extra-virgin olive oil

3 large egg yolks, at room temperature

1 tablespoon fresh lemon juice

Freshly ground black pepper

4 medium artichokes

½ lemon

To make the aioli, in a mortar with a pestle, grind together the garlic and salt, working in a circular motion, until a paste forms. Measure the oil into a container with a spout.

In a large bowl, whisk the egg yolks until blended. While whisking gently, very slowly drizzle in the oil, ½ teaspoon at a time, until a thick emulsion forms (after about 2 tablespoons oil have been added). Now begin whisking in the oil about 1 teaspoon at a time until all the oil is incorporated. (Alternatively, using an electric mixer on medium-low speed, beat the egg yolks briefly just until blended. Then, with the mixer on medium-high speed, very slowly drizzle in the oil, a few drops at a time. Once an emulsion forms, begin streaming in the oil more quickly, stopping to scrape down the sides of the bowl just before all of the oil has been added.) Gently stir in the garlic paste and lemon juice. Season with pepper. Use right away, or refrigerate in an airtight container for up to 5 days.

Working with 1 artichoke at a time, trim the stem even with the base. Snap off the small, tough leaves around the base. Using a sharp chef's or serrated knife, cut off the top one-third of the artichoke, then snip off any remaining prickly leaf tips with kitchen scissors. Cut each artichoke in half lengthwise. Using a small metal spoon, scoop out and discard the fuzzy choke. Rub the cut surfaces of the artichoke halves with the lemon half to prevent them from turning brown.

Select a wide saucepan large enough to hold the artichokes in a single layer. Place a steamer rack in the saucepan and add water to reach the bottom of the rack. Place the artichokes, cut side down, on the rack. Bring the water to a simmer over medium heat. Cover and cook until the base of an artichoke half is easily pierced with a fork, about 20 minutes.

Serve warm, at room temperature, or chilled on individual plates, accompanied with the aioli.

Gougères

Gougère is just a fancy French word for cheese puff. Originally from Burgundy, where they often accompany wine tastings in local cellars, these savory bites made from choux pastry are the perfect accompaniment to a glass—or three—of wine in a Parisian café any time of day. "I can't believe I'm drinking before noon," says Emily. "It's okay. This is Sancerre. It's a breakfast wine," responds Mindy.

makes about 48 puffs

2 cups plus 2 tablespoons whole milk

½ cup unsalted butter, cut into pieces

2 teaspoons fine sea salt

2 cups all-purpose flour

8 large eggs

½ lb Gruyère or Comté cheese, finely shredded

Position 2 racks in the center of the oven and preheat the oven to 375°F. Line 2 sheet pans with parchment paper.

In a heavy saucepan over high heat, combine 2 cups of the milk, the butter, and salt and bring to a boil. Add the flour all at once, reduce the heat to low, and stir with a wooden spoon until the mixture forms a ball and pulls cleanly away from the sides of the pan, about 5 minutes. Remove from the heat and let cool for 2 minutes.

Using an electric mixer on medium speed, add the eggs, one at a time, beating well after each addition until thoroughly incorporated and the dough is smooth and shiny; this step should take about 5 minutes. Stir in three-fourths of the cheese, distributing it evenly.

Transfer the dough to a pastry bag fitted with a large round tip. Pipe mounds about 2 inches in diameter onto the prepared sheet pans, spacing them about 2 inches apart. You should have about 48 puffs. Brush the mounds with the remaining 2 tablespoons milk, then sprinkle evenly with the remaining cheese.

Bake the pastries, switching the pans between the racks and rotating them back to front about halfway through baking, until well puffed and golden brown, 30–35 minutes. Let the pastries cool briefly on the pans on wire racks and serve warm, or let cool completely and serve at room temperature. Leftover pastries will keep in an airtight container in the refrigerator for up to 5 days.

20-Euro Caesar Salad

Emily is sitting in the Café de Flore having a glass of wine when she strikes up a conversation with Thomas, a provocative Frenchman seated at the adjoining table. "Do you think he's her son or her lover?" asks Thomas after seeing Emily watching a couple at a nearby table. "Oh, um, I . . . I was just watching to see if the Caesar salad is really worth 20 euros!" They bet on who is correct, with the loser buying the next bottle of wine, and end up back at Emily's apartment. Was the salad worth it?

makes 4 servings

2 cups cubed coarse country bread, in 1-inch cubes

6 tablespoons extra-virgin olive oil

Fine sea salt and freshly ground black pepper

1 large clove garlic, chopped

3 olive oil–packed anchovy fillets, or more to taste

2 large egg yolks

2 tablespoons fresh lemon juice

1 teaspoon Dijon mustard

1 teaspoon Worcestershire sauce

1/3 cup neutral oil, such as avocado oil

2 hearts romaine lettuce, separated into individual leaves

Parmesan cheese for shaving

Preheat the oven to 375°F. Pile the bread cubes onto a sheet pan. Drizzle with 3 tablespoons of the olive oil, season with salt and pepper, and toss to coat, then spread the cubes in a single layer. Bake the cubes, turning once or twice, until golden on all sides, about 13 minutes. Set aside to cool.

In a bowl, using a fork, mash together the garlic and 1/4 teaspoon salt until a paste forms. Mash the anchovies into the paste. (Alternatively, use a mortar and pestle to mash the garlic, salt, and anchovies.) Whisk in the egg yolks, lemon juice, mustard, Worcestershire sauce, and 1/4 teaspoon pepper until blended. While whisking constantly, gradually add the remaining 3 tablespoons olive oil and then the avocado oil in a thin stream, continuing to whisk until the dressing is smooth. You will need only about half of the dressing for the salad. The remainder will keep in an airtight container in the refrigerator for up to three days and can be used on a second Caesar or a simple green salad.

In a wide serving bowl, combine the lettuce and half of the croutons. Drizzle with about half of the dressing and mix gently but thoroughly. Top with the remaining croutons. Using a vegetable peeler, shave the cheese over the salad. Serve at once.

Salade Niçoise

Although this pretty composed salad originated in southern France, it is familiar fare on café and bistro menus in Paris and is a popular choice for Emily when she heads out for a gossipy, wine-heavy lunch with Mindy or her coworkers. In this version, the finest-quality olive oil–packed tuna you can find is served alongside a riot of ingredients—Niçoise olives, tomatoes, haricots verts, potatoes, hard-cooked eggs—all arranged atop lettuce leaves and dressed with a tangy vinaigrette.

makes 4 servings

4 large eggs

1 lb small yellow or red potatoes

Fine sea salt and freshly ground black pepper

1 lb haricots verts, stem ends trimmed

1 head butter lettuce, leaves separated

4 tomatoes, quartered

2 (7-oz) cans olive oil–packed tuna, drained

1/2 cup Niçoise olives

8 olive oil–packed anchovy fillets (optional)

VINAIGRETTE

2 tablespoons red wine vinegar

1 teaspoon Dijon mustard

1/4 cup extra-virgin olive oil

Chopped fresh tarragon leaves, for garnish (optional)

To hard-cook the eggs, put them into a saucepan just large enough to hold them. Add cold water to cover by 1 inch and bring just to a boil over high heat. Remove the pan from the heat, cover, and let stand for 15 minutes. Have ready a bowl filled with ice water. After 15 minutes, drain the eggs, immerse them in the ice water, and let cool.

Meanwhile, in a second saucepan, combine the potatoes with water to cover by 1 inch and 1 tablespoon salt. Bring to a boil over medium-high heat, reduce the heat to medium, and cook, stirring occasionally, until tender when pierced with a fork, about 20 minutes. Remove from the heat and, using a slotted spoon, transfer the potatoes to a colander, rinse under cold running water until cool enough to handle, and then transfer to a cutting board and cut into halves or quarters.

Return the pan to the stove top and bring the water to a boil over high heat. Add the haricots verts and cook until crisp-tender, 3–4 minutes. Drain the beans into the colander, rinse under cold running water, and drain well.

Peel the hard-cooked eggs and cut in half lengthwise. Arrange the lettuce leaves on individual plates. Make small mounds of the haricots verts, potatoes, tomatoes, tuna, olives, and egg halves on and around the lettuce, dividing the ingredients evenly among the plates. Top each mound of potatoes with 2 anchovy fillets, if using.

To make the vinaigrette, in a small bowl, whisk together the vinegar and mustard, then whisk in the oil until emulsified. Season with salt and pepper. Drizzle the salad with the vinaigrette and season with salt and pepper. Garnish with the tarragon, if using, and serve.

Salade Frisée aux Lardons

On her second day at Savoir—after meeting Mindy for the first time in the Jardin du Palais Royal—Emily returns to the office only to encounter her coworkers enjoying lunch at the bistro next door. As she eyes the salads, wine bottles, and cigarettes covering the table, she feels the sting of being left out. No doubt at least one of her coworkers was enjoying this classic bistro salad of lacey frisée tossed in a shallot vinaigrette and topped with crisp bacon and poached eggs.

makes 4 servings

4 thick-cut bacon slices, cut into ½-inch pieces

VINAIGRETTE

2 tablespoons red wine vinegar or sherry vinegar

1 tablespoon minced shallot

1 teaspoon Dijon mustard

3 tablespoons extra-virgin olive oil

Fine sea salt and freshly ground black pepper

2 heads frisée, pale inner leaves only, leaves separated and torn into bite-size pieces

4 large eggs

Line a large plate with paper towels. In a frying pan over medium-high heat, fry the bacon, turning the pieces once or twice, until crisp, 6–7 minutes. Using a slotted spoon, transfer to the towel-lined plate to drain. Set aside.

To make the vinaigrette, in a large bowl, whisk together the vinegar, shallot, and mustard. Whisk in the oil until emulsified and season with salt and pepper.

Add the frisée and bacon to the bowl and toss to coat evenly with the vinaigrette. Divide the salad among four individual salad plates.

Line a small plate with paper towels. In a large frying pan over medium-high heat, add water to a depth of 1 inch and bring just to a simmer over medium-high heat. Crack an egg into a small bowl and slide the egg into the water. Working quickly, repeat with the remaining 3 eggs. Gently spoon the simmering water over the eggs and cook until the whites are just opaque and a thin film forms over the yolks, about 4 minutes.

Using a slotted spoon, remove each egg from the water, blot the bottom on the towel-lined plate, and then carefully transfer the egg to a salad, gently sliding it on top. Season the eggs with salt and pepper and serve the salads at once.

Soupe au Pistou

Heavily laden with vegetables and small pasta, this soup is the French equivalent of Italian minestrone. The addition of *pistou*, a sauce similar to basil pesto but without nuts and cheese, gives the soup its deep, rich flavor. To save time, purchased basil pesto is used here. The canned beans are also a time-saver. But if fresh shelling beans, such as cranberry or butter beans, are in the market, use them in their place.

makes 6 servings

1 tablespoon extra-virgin olive oil

1 small yellow onion, finely chopped

Fine sea salt and freshly ground black pepper

1 small leek, white and tender green parts, quartered lengthwise and thinly sliced crosswise

1 large carrot, peeled and diced

2 celery ribs, diced

1 can (14 oz) diced tomatoes with juices

3 cups chicken broth

2 cups water

2 cans (15 oz each) white beans, such as Great Northern or cannellini, drained

1 large zucchini, trimmed and diced

4 fresh thyme sprigs

4 fresh flat-leaf parsley sprigs

½ lb haricots verts or green beans, stem ends trimmed and cut into 1-inch lengths

½ cup soup pasta, such as small shells or macaroni

1 cup store-bought basil pesto

In a large saucepan or soup pot over medium-high heat, warm the oil. Add the onion and a pinch of salt and cook, stirring often, until golden brown, about 5 minutes. Add the leek, carrot, and celery and cook, stirring often, until slightly softened, about 3 minutes. Add the tomatoes and cook, stirring, until they have cooked down slightly, about 5 minutes. Add the broth, water, beans, zucchini, thyme, and parsley and stir to combine. Season with salt and bring to a boil. Reduce the heat to low, cover partially, and simmer until the vegetables are tender and the flavors come together, 30–45 minutes. If the soup thickens too much, add more liquid to thin to a good consistency.

Add the haricots verts and pasta to the pot and cook until the pasta is al dente and the haricots verts are tender, 8–10 minutes.

Remove and discard the thyme and parsley sprigs. Taste and adjust the seasoning with salt and pepper. Stir in 2 tablespoons of the pesto. Divide the soup among warmed individual bowls and top each serving with a big dollop of pesto. Serve at once.

French Onion Soup

A big bowl of French onion soup is as warm as a big hug from a friend— or from a cute French chef named Gabriel. Take the time to caramelize the onions slowly so they become jammy, sweet, and richly browned. A couple of thick slices of toasted French bread topped with melted Gruyère give the soup gooey decadence. Use the best-quality beef stock you can find—or better yet, make your own.

makes 6–8 servings

SOUP

6 tablespoons unsalted butter

1 tablespoon extra-virgin olive oil

2 lb yellow onions, very thinly sliced

½ teaspoon sugar

½ teaspoon fine sea salt

1½ teaspoons all-purpose flour

8 cups beef broth

2 cups water

1 cup dry white wine

½ teaspoon freshly ground black pepper

TOASTS

12–16 baguette slices, each ½ inch thick

2 cloves garlic, halved

3 tablespoons extra-virgin olive oil

2 cups shredded Gruyère
or Emmentaler cheese

2 tablespoons unsalted butter,
cut into small pieces

To make the soup, in a large, heavy saucepan over medium heat, melt the butter with the oil. When the butter foams, stir in the onions and cook, stirring often, until translucent, 4–5 minutes. Reduce the heat to low, cover, and cook until the onions are lightly golden, about 15 minutes. Uncover and sprinkle with the sugar and salt. Raise the heat to medium and cook uncovered, stirring often, until the onions are deep golden brown, 30–40 minutes.

Sprinkle the flour over the onions and cook, stirring, until the flour browns, 2–3 minutes. While stirring constantly, gradually pour in the broth and water. Raise the heat to high and bring to a boil. Stir in the wine and pepper, then reduce the heat to low, cover, and cook until the onions begin to fall apart, about 45 minutes.

Meanwhile, make the toasts. Preheat the broiler. Arrange the bread slices in a single layer on a sheet pan and place under the broiler. Toast, turning once, until crunchy but not browned, 2–4 minutes. Remove the pan from the oven, rub the bread slices on both sides with the garlic, and then brush on both sides with the oil. Return the bread to the oven and broil, turning once, until golden on both sides, 2–4 minutes.

Preheat the oven to 450°F. Ladle the soup into 6–8 ovenproof bowls, filling to no more than ½ inch of the rim. Place the bowls on a sheet pan. Top the bowls with the toasted bread slices, dividing them evenly. Sprinkle the bread slices evenly with the cheese and dot with the butter.

Bake until a golden crust forms on the top of each bowl and the soup bubbles around the edges, about 15 minutes. Serve at once.

Provençal Eggplant & Tomato Gratin

After visiting the country market while staying at Camille's family's château, Gabriel makes an exquisite meal of coq au vin (page 98) and grilled *aubergine*—aka eggplant—to which Emily announces she is allergic. With any luck, you don't share Emily's allergy and can enjoy *aubergine* in all its guises, including in this light gratin. Try this recipe at the peak of summer when tomatoes and eggplants are at their ripest and most flavorful.

makes 6–8 servings

2 Italian eggplants, about 1 lb total weight

Fine sea salt and freshly ground black pepper

Extra-virgin olive oil, for brushing

6 ripe, juicy tomatoes, about 3 lb total weight

1 clove garlic, minced

1 teaspoon fresh thyme leaves

¼ cup chopped fresh basil

¼ cup dried coarse bread crumbs

1 tablespoon unsalted butter, cut into small pieces

Trim off the stem and blossom ends from each eggplant and cut the eggplants crosswise into slices ½-inch-thick. Lightly salt the eggplant slices on both sides and arrange them on paper towels. Let sit for 30 minutes.

Preheat the oven to 400°F. Blot the eggplant slices dry with a paper towel. Arrange the slices in a single layer on a sheet pan. Brush the slices on both sides with oil and then season both sides with pepper.

Bake the eggplant slices until the underside of each slice is lightly browned and a crust has formed on the top, about 15 minutes. Turn over the slices and continue to bake until soft when pierced with a knife tip and the underside is browned, about 10 minutes longer. Remove from the oven.

Meanwhile, coarsely chop the tomatoes and transfer them and all their juices to a bowl. Add ½ teaspoon salt, ¼ teaspoon pepper, and the garlic and thyme and toss to combine.

Raise the oven temperature to 450°F. Brush the bottom and sides of a 14-inch oval gratin dish with oil.

Arrange the eggplant slices, slightly overlapping, in a single layer in the prepared gratin dish. Sprinkle with half the basil. Spread the tomato mixture evenly over the eggplant, lifting the slices a little to let the juices run underneath. Sprinkle evenly with the bread crumbs and dot with the butter.

Bake until the tomatoes are bubbling and the bread crumbs are browned, 20–25 minutes. Sprinkle the gratin with the remaining basil and serve at once.

Cassoulet

Cassoulet is an event. An epic mixture of duck confit, sausages, and creamy white beans, it is perfect for a celebratory dinner party—with plenty of French wine, of course. This is a shortened version of the more complex traditional recipe, but it is still exceedingly delicious. You can forgo the duck confit, purchase it from a well-stocked butcher, or make it up to 1 month in advance and store the cooked whole legs submerged in duck fat in the refrigerator until needed, then bring them to room temperature before pulling the meat and skin from the bones.

makes 6 servings

DUCK CONFIT

3 tablespoons kosher salt

1 teaspoon black peppercorns, crushed

2 tablespoons minced shallot

1 teaspoon chopped garlic

1 teaspoon fresh thyme leaves

1 bay leaf, crumbled

4 duck legs

5 cups rendered duck or goose fat, melted

continued on next page

To make the duck confit, in a small bowl, stir together the salt, peppercorns, shallot, garlic, thyme, and bay leaf. Place the duck legs in a single layer in a 9×13-inch baking dish. Sprinkle the salt mixture evenly over the duck legs, turning them several times as you do to coat evenly. Cover the dish with plastic wrap. Top with a weight or two, such as heavy roasting pan or bricks wrapped in aluminum foil. Refrigerate overnight.

Preheat the oven to 275°F. Remove the duck legs from the dry brine, rinse under cold running water, and pat dry with paper towels. Rinse and dry the baking dish and place it on a sheet pan. Return the duck legs to the dish and pour the duck fat over them, covering them completely. Cook until the meat pulls away from the bone, about 2½ hours.

Transfer the duck legs to a cutting board. Strain the fat through a fine-mesh sieve into a heatproof, airtight container and let cool completely. When the duck is cool enough to handle, remove the skin and set aside. Pull the meat from the bones, tearing it into 2-inch pieces. (If making ahead, store the skin, meat, and fat separately in airtight containers in the refrigerator for up to 3 days.)

continued on next page

continued from page 27

BEANS

2 cups dried Tarbais or cannellini beans, picked over and soaked overnight in water to cover

2 whole cloves

1 yellow onion, halved

8 cups water

Kosher salt and freshly ground black pepper

½ lb skinless pork belly, in one piece

2 carrots, peeled and halved lengthwise

1 celery rib, halved crosswise

4 cloves garlic, lightly crushed

1 bay leaf

1 small yellow onion, finely chopped

4 cloves garlic, minced

1 can (14 oz) crushed tomatoes with juices

1 lb fresh pork sausages, such as Toulouse or sweet Italian

2 cups fresh bread crumbs

To make the beans, drain the beans into a colander and rinse with cold running water. Stick the cloves into the onion halves. In a 4- to 5-quart Dutch oven or other heavy pot over medium-high heat, combine the beans and water; discard any beans that float. Add 1 teaspoon salt, the pork belly, carrots, celery, onion halves, garlic, and bay leaf and bring to a boil. Adjust the heat to maintain a gentle simmer and cook uncovered, stirring occasionally, until the beans are tender, 1–1½ hours. The timing will depend on the age of the beans. Remove from the heat. Scoop out and discard the carrots, celery, onion, garlic, and bay leaf. Transfer the pork belly to a cutting board and cut into ¼-inch pieces. Reserve cooking liquid.

In a large frying pan over medium-high heat, warm 2 tablespoons of the reserved duck fat. Add the chopped onion and cook, stirring occasionally, until golden, about 8 minutes. Add the minced garlic and pork belly and cook for 1 minute longer. Add the tomatoes, ½ teaspoon salt, ½ teaspoon pepper, and about 1 cup of the bean cooking liquid. Reduce the heat to low, cover, and simmer until the flavors are blended, about 15 minutes. Using a slotted spoon, transfer the beans to the frying pan and stir to combine. Transfer the bean cooking liquid to a bowl and reserve. Rinse and dry the Dutch oven.

Preheat the oven to 350°F.

In the Dutch oven over low heat, warm the duck skin, turning as needed, until crisp and browned, about 15 minutes. Using the slotted spoon, transfer to a plate. Add the sausages to the Dutch oven, raise the heat to medium, and cook, turning occasionally, until nicely browned all over, about 5–10 minutes. Transfer to a cutting board, let cool briefly, and cut into ½-inch-thick slices. Add the bread crumbs to the Dutch oven and cook, stirring, until lightly toasted. Transfer to a small bowl. Wipe out the Dutch oven.

Add one-third of the bean mixture to the Dutch oven. Top with half each of the duck meat and sausage slices. Add half of the remaining bean mixture, then top with the remaining duck meat and sausage. Top with the remaining bean mixture and about 1 cup of the reserved liquid. Place on the stove top over medium-high heat and bring to a boil.

Sprinkle the cassoulet evenly with about one-fourth of the bread crumbs, cover, transfer to the oven, and bake until the crumbs are lightly browned, about 30 minutes. Using a spoon, break up the crust, then sprinkle the top with another one-fourth of the bread crumbs, cover, and return to the oven for 30 minutes. Repeat twice, ladling some of the reserved bean liquid over the top of the cassoulet if it is drying out, and continue to bake until the final layer of bread crumbs is lightly browned, about 1 hour longer. The total oven cooking time is 2 hours.

Remove the cassoulet from the oven and let rest for about 15 minutes. Garnish with the crumbled crisped duck skin before serving.

Roast Chicken with Haricot Verts

Emily's lunch meeting with Durée Cosmetics CMO Olivia Thompson goes sideways when she asks Emily to become an influencer for Durée and refuses to return to Savoir because Sylvie still works there. Sylvie, unhappy about the lunch, tells Emily to deactivate her Instagram account, which she does—but only for a little while! A lunch of rotisserie-roasted chicken is a common sight in the streets of Paris, but when you can't have lunch in Paris or swing by a butcher for a fresh-roasted bird, this easy recipe is the next best thing.

—◊—

makes 4–6 servings

ROAST CHICKEN

4 tablespoons unsalted butter, at room temperature

¼ cup fresh lemon juice

1 tablespoon chopped fresh rosemary, tarragon, or thyme

3 cloves garlic, minced

¼ teaspoon sweet paprika

Fine sea salt and freshly ground black pepper

1 whole chicken, about 5 lb

Olive oil, for the pan

HARICOTS VERTS

1½ lb haricots verts, stem ends trimmed

2 tablespoons extra-virgin olive oil

1 shallot, minced

1 teaspoon finely grated lemon zest

Fine sea salt and freshly ground black pepper

1 tablespoon finely chopped fresh flat-leaf parsley

To make the chicken, preheat the oven to 425°F. In a small bowl, using a fork, mix together the butter, lemon juice, rosemary, garlic, paprika, and a pinch each salt and pepper until evenly blended.

Pat the chicken dry with paper towels. Starting near the cavity of the chicken, slip your fingers between the skin and the flesh, loosening the skin on the breasts and being careful not to tear it. Spread about half of the butter mixture over the flesh. Then spread the remaining butter mixture over the entire outside of the bird. Oil a cast-iron frying pan just large enough to hold the chicken. Place the bird, breast side up, in the pan. Roast the chicken, basting several times with the pan juices, until golden brown and the juices run clear when a thigh is pierced with a knife, 45–50 minutes. An instant-read thermometer inserted into the thickest part of a thigh (but not touching bone) should register 170°F. Let rest for 10 minutes before carving.

While the chicken is resting, make the haricots verts. Bring a large saucepan three-fourths full of water to a boil. Meanwhile, fill a large bowl with ice water. Add the beans to the boiling water and cook until bright green and tender but still slightly resistant to the bite, 5–7 minutes. Drain the beans, then plunge them into the ice water to stop the cooking. Drain well and set aside.

In a large frying pan over medium heat, warm the oil. Add the shallot and cook, stirring often, until softened, about 2 minutes. Raise the heat to medium-high, add the haricots verts, and cook, stirring occasionally, just until they begin to brown, about 2 minutes. Stir in the lemon zest and cook, stirring, for 30–60 seconds longer. Remove from the heat and season with salt and pepper. Transfer the beans to a warmed serving dish and garnish with the parsley.

Carve the chicken and serve with the haricots verts alongside.

Steak Frites

Bistro-style *frites*, or French fries, are an ideal partner to a juicy, seared steak, especially when the steak is topped with a simple shallot-herb butter. This irresistible combination is a standard—and much loved—menu item throughout Paris. The secret to great *frites* is to fry the potatoes twice, the first time to cook their interior and the second time to create a golden, crispy exterior. Fry them the second time while the steak rests and your timing will be *magnifique*!

makes 4 servings

Pomme Frites (page 211)

STEAKS

2 large boneless strip steaks, each 12–16 oz and 1 inch thick, halved crosswise

Kosher salt and freshly ground black pepper

4 tablespoons unsalted butter, at room temperature

1 small shallot, minced

1 tablespoon minced fresh flat-leaf parsley

1 clove garlic, minced

1 tablespoon canola oil

Prepare the frites as directed, frying once, up to 2 hours in advance.

To make the steaks, generously season the steaks on both sides with salt and pepper. In a small bowl, using a fork, mix together the butter, shallot, parsley, and garlic until evenly blended. Set aside.

Heat a large cast-iron frying pan over medium-high heat until hot. Add the oil, swirl the pan to coat the bottom, and then add the steaks. Cook, turning once, until well browned and done to your liking, about 4 minutes on each side for medium-rare (the steak should register 125°F on an instant-read thermometer). Transfer the steaks to a warmed platter, tent with aluminum foil, and rest for 10 minutes while you finish the frites.

Reheat the oil for the frites to 370°F. Fry the potatoes in batches the second time as directed, then drain and transfer to the fresh paper towels. When all the potatoes are fried, transfer them to a plate or shallow serving bowl and season generously with salt.

Transfer the steaks to warmed individual plates, top each steak with one-fourth of the shallot butter, and serve with the frites alongside.

Beef Bourguignon

A hearty winter stew that is at home in any French bistro, *boeuf bourguignon* represents French country cooking at its best. Tough cuts of beef are transformed into a melt-in-your mouth *tour de force*. The addition of plenty of wine, ideally something from Burgundy, creates the rich sauce to which mushrooms and pearl onions are added. Serve with mashed potatoes, egg noodles, or crusty French bread for soaking up the deliciously rich sauce.

makes 6–8 servings

3½ lb boneless beef chuck roast, cut into 2-inch cubes

Fine sea salt and freshly ground black pepper

¼ cup all-purpose flour

6 oz thick-cut bacon slices, cut into 1-inch pieces

1 large carrot, peeled and sliced

1 yellow onion, finely chopped

3 cups dry red wine, such as a Burgundy Pinot Noir

20–24 frozen peeled pearl onions

2 cloves garlic, minced

1 tablespoon fresh thyme leaves, or 1½ teaspoons dried thyme

1 bay leaf

1 tablespoon tomato paste

3 tablespoons unsalted butter, plus more if needed

1 lb cremini or white mushrooms, brushed clean and thickly sliced

Chopped fresh flat-leaf parsley leaves, for garnish

Sprinkle the beef cubes on all sides with ½ teaspoon salt and ¼ teaspoon pepper. Spread the flour on a large plate. Working in small batches, lightly coat the beef cubes with flour, shaking off the excess. Set aside.

In a Dutch oven or other heavy pot over low heat, fry the bacon, stirring occasionally, until crisp and golden, 4–5 minutes. Using a slotted spoon, transfer the bacon to a bowl. Raise the heat to medium-high and, working in batches, brown the meat, turning once, until well browned on two sides, about 5 minutes. Transfer to the bowl with the bacon. When all the meat has been browned, add the carrot and onion and cook, stirring occasionally, until browned, about 5 minutes. Transfer to the bowl with the bacon and meat.

Pour off the fat from the pot. Reduce the heat to medium, add the wine, and deglaze the pot, scraping the pot bottom with a wooden spoon to dislodge any browned bits. Stir in the reserved beef mixture, pearl onions, garlic, thyme, bay leaf, tomato paste, ½ teaspoon salt, and ¼ teaspoon pepper and bring to a simmer. Reduce the heat to low, cover, and simmer gently, stirring occasionally, until the meat is very tender, 2½–3 hours.

While the meat cooks, in a large frying pan over medium heat, melt the butter. When the butter foams, add the mushrooms and cook, stirring occasionally, until lightly browned, 4–5 minutes. Remove from the heat.

When the beef is tender, add the mushrooms to the stew and simmer until warmed through, about 10 minutes.

Using the slotted spoon, transfer the stew solids to a bowl, removing and discarding the bay leaf. Using a large metal spoon, skim the fat from the surface of the cooking liquid. Raise the heat to medium-high, bring to a boil, and cook until the liquid thickens slightly, 1–2 minutes. Return the stew solids to the pot, stir well, and remove from the heat.

Spoon the stew into warmed shallow individual bowls, garnish with the parsley, and serve.

Profiteroles au Chocolat

These little filled choux puffs make an elegant end to any Parisian meal, and they are easy to assemble in stages. Make and bake the puffs ahead of time, then freeze them for up to 2 weeks. Warm them in a 375°F oven just until thawed and crisp, let cool, and then fill with the ice cream. To make cream puffs, bake slightly larger mounds of dough, then, using a piping bag, fill each puff with pastry cream (page 213) and dip the top in the chocolate sauce. *C'est vraiment délicieux!*

makes 10–12 servings

CHOUX PUFFS

½ cup whole milk

½ cup water

6 tablespoons unsalted butter, cut into pieces

¼ teaspoon fine sea salt

1 cup all-purpose flour

4 large eggs, beaten

CHOCOLATE SAUCE

6 oz bittersweet chocolate, chopped

⅓ cup light corn syrup

⅓ cup whole milk

1 tablespoon unsalted butter

1 teaspoon pure vanilla extract

1 quart ice cream, such as vanilla, salted caramel, or pistachio

To make the puffs, position 2 racks in the center of the oven and preheat the oven to 425°F. Line 2 sheet pans with parchment paper.

In a heavy saucepan over medium-high heat, combine the milk, water, butter, and salt and bring to a boil. When the butter melts, remove the pan from the heat, add the flour all at once, and stir vigorously with a wooden spoon until blended. Return the pan to medium heat and continue stirring until the mixture forms a ball and pulls cleanly away from the sides of the pan, about 1 minute. Remove from the heat and let cool for 3–4 minutes.

Using an electric mixer on medium-high speed, add the beaten eggs, one-fourth at a time, beating well after each addition until thoroughly incorporated and the dough is smooth and shiny. Let the dough cool for 10 minutes.

Transfer the dough to a piping bag fitted with a ³/₁₆-inch round tip. Pipe mounds about 1 inch in diameter (about 1 teaspoon dough) onto the prepared sheet pans, spacing them about 2 inches apart. You should have about 40 puffs.

Bake the puffs for 15 minutes, then reduce the oven temperature to 375°F and continue baking until well puffed and golden brown, about 5 minutes. Remove from the oven and immediately prick the bottom of each puff with a thin wooden skewer or toothpick. Return to the oven, leave the oven door open, and allow the puffs to dry out for about 15 minutes. Then remove from the oven and let the pastries cool completely on the pans on wire racks.

continued on page 40

continued from page 38

To make the chocolate sauce, combine the chocolate and corn syrup in a heatproof bowl and set over (not touching) barely simmering water in a saucepan. Heat, stirring often, until the chocolate melts. Add the milk, butter, and vanilla and stir until blended. Remove from over the heat.

Slice each puff in half horizontally, stopping just short of the opposite side. (The puff should open like a clam shell.) Place a small scoop of ice cream in the bottom half of each puff and replace the top. Arrange the filled puffs on individual plates. Top with the chocolate sauce and serve right away.

Orange Crème Caramel

Dessert and wine at the end of a leisurely French meal is a treat, even if it's with your coworkers. When Emily gets retweeted by Brigitte Macron, the French president's wife, in episode 2, she finally gets acknowledgment (and congratulations) from Paul Brossard, Savoir's former owner, and from her coworkers, who invite her to join them at the bistro where they are finishing up a long lunch. Even Sylvie seems mildly impressed. _Crème caramel_, a creamy baked custard bathed in caramel, makes a fine _fin_ to this lunch or any French meal.

makes 6 servings

2 cups sugar

½ cup water

1¾ cups heavy cream

¾ cup whole milk

2 teaspoons finely grated orange zest

4 large egg yolks plus 1 large whole egg

2 tablespoons orange liqueur, such as Grand Marnier

Pinch of fine sea salt

Preheat the oven to 325°F. Place six ¾-cup ramekins in a 9×13-inch baking dish.

In a heavy saucepan, combine 1½ cups of the sugar and the water. Cover and bring to a simmer over medium-high heat, checking the sugar often. Once the sugar starts to melt, uncover and gently swirl the pan occasionally until the sugar dissolves, about 5 minutes. Continue to simmer, uncovered, until the sugar turns a deep amber, 4–6 minutes. Moving quickly but carefully, pour the caramel into the ramekins, dividing it evenly. Tilt each ramekin to coat the bottom and sides evenly with the caramel.

In another saucepan over medium-high heat, combine the cream, milk, and orange zest and bring to a simmer. Cover and set aside for 30 minutes to steep. In a large bowl, whisk together the remaining ½ cup sugar, egg yolks and whole egg, orange liqueur, and salt until blended. Slowly whisk the warm cream mixture into the egg mixture until combined.

Pour the egg-cream mixture through a fine-mesh sieve into a pitcher, then pour the mixture into the ramekins, dividing it evenly. Transfer the baking dish to the center oven rack and pour hot water into the dish to come halfway up the sides of the ramekins. Bake the custards until set but the centers still jiggle slightly in the center when the ramekins are gently shaken, about 35 minutes.

Carefully remove the baking dish from the oven and let the custards cool in the water bath for 30 minutes. Remove the ramekins from the water bath, cover each ramekin with plastic wrap, and refrigerate for at least 6 hours or up to 3 days.

To unmold each custard, run a knife around the inside edge of each ramekin to loosen the custard, invert a dessert plate over the ramekin, invert the ramekin and plate together, and lift off the ramekin, releasing the custard and its caramel onto the plate. Serve chilled.

DEUX
LA BRASSERIE

Smoked Salmon Crème Fraîche Hors d'Oeuvres

Sylvie begrudgingly invites Emily to the launch party for De L'Heure, a new scent being released by Antoine Lambert's perfumery Maison Lavaux. At the beginning of the party, we see Emily cramming as many little smoked salmon and shrimp hors d'oeuvres into her mouth as she can before being chastised by Sylvie. These easy-to-make bites have a real pop of flavor and make excellent passed appetizers at any party.

makes about 24 pieces

1 English cucumber, 12 inches long

½ cup crème fraîche

2 teaspoons fresh lemon juice

¼ lb sliced cold-smoked salmon

2 tablespoons minced fresh flat-leaf parsley or dill

Freshly ground black pepper

Trim the ends off the cucumber and peel if desired. Cut crosswise into about twenty-four ½-inch-thick slices and arrange on a serving platter.

In a small bowl, stir together the crème fraîche and lemon juice. Cut the salmon into as many pieces as cucumber slices.

Top each cucumber slice with a piece of the salmon and top the salmon with 1 teaspoon of the crème fraîche mixture. Garnish with the parsley and pepper and serve.

Tapenade Provençale

Tapenade, a mix of olives, anchovies, capers, and garlic, delivers a burst of salty-briny flavor that will have you dreaming of the sunny climes of southern France. Spread it on toasted baguette slices and pair it with a sturdy rosé from Provence or a full-bodied Vouvray from the Loire for your next coworkers' get-together.

makes 24 pieces

TAPENADE

1½ cups pitted mild green olives, such as Lucques or Picholines, or black Niçoise olives, or a combination

3 olive oil–packed anchovy fillets, rinsed and patted dry

3 tablespoons capers, rinsed

1½ tablespoons coarsely chopped fresh flat-leaf parsley

2 cloves garlic, finely chopped

1 tablespoon fresh lemon juice

¼ teaspoon freshly ground black pepper

⅓ cup extra-virgin olive oil

24 thin baguette slices

Extra-virgin olive oil, for brushing

Narrow roasted red pepper strips, for garnish (optional)

Flat-leaf parsley leaves, for garnish (optional)

To make the tapenade, in a food processor, combine the olives, anchovies, capers, parsley, garlic, lemon juice, and pepper and pulse once or twice until roughly mixed. Add the oil and pulse briefly, stopping to scrape down the bowl sides once or twice. The texture should be slightly chunky rather than a smooth purée. Set aside. (The tapenade can be transferred to an airtight container and refrigerated for up to 48 hours. Return to room temperature for 15 minutes before serving.)

Preheat the oven to 350°F. Lightly brush the baguette slices on both sides with oil and arrange in a single layer on a sheet pan. Bake until golden, 10–15 minutes.

Transfer the toasted baguette slices to a serving platter. Spread each one with about 1 tablespoon of the tapenade. If desired, garnish with roasted red pepper and parsley. Serve warm or at room temperature.

Pissaladière

Pissaladière, a savory tart that originated in Nice, stars anchovies and olives atop a sweet, tender bed of caramelized onions. Although it is traditionally made with a yeasted dough, Julia Child, America's own "French chef," preferred puff pastry. This easy version follows her lead with store-bought puff pastry. For the best outcome, choose an all-butter pastry.

makes 8–10 servings

¼ cup olive oil

3 lb yellow or sweet onions, halved and thinly sliced

1 teaspoon chopped fresh thyme leaves, or ½ teaspoon dried thyme

Fine sea salt and freshly ground black pepper

2 sheets frozen puff pastry, about 1 lb total weight

All-purpose flour, for the work surface

1 large egg

1 tablespoon water

About 24 olive oil–packed anchovy fillets, rinsed and patted dry

About 1 cup pitted and halved Niçoise or other black olives

Fresh basil leaves, for garnish (optional)

In a large frying pan over medium-low heat, warm the oil. Add the onions and thyme and season with salt and pepper. Cover and cook gently, stirring occasionally, until caramelized and very tender, about 30 minutes. Uncover the pan and cook until all the excess moisture has evaporated, about 5 minutes longer. Let cool.

While the onions cook, remove the puff pastry from the packaging and thaw for 30 minutes at room temperature.

Position 2 racks in the center of the oven and preheat the oven to 400°F. Line 2 large sheet pans with parchment paper. On a lightly floured work surface, roll out a puff pastry sheet to a ¼-inch thickness. Cut into 2 rectangles. Transfer them to a prepared sheet pan. Repeat with the second pastry sheet and transfer to the second sheet pan. (If the puff pastry came as a single sheet, cut it in 4 rectangles and roll out each as directed.)

In a small bowl, using a fork, stir together the egg and water until blended. Lightly brush each pastry sheet with the egg mixture. Spread half of the onion mixture over each pastry sheet, leaving a ½-inch border on all sides. Decoratively arrange half of the anchovy fillets and half of the olives on each pastry sheet.

Bake the tarts, switching the pans between the racks and rotating them back to front about halfway through baking, until the edges are golden brown, about 30 minutes. Transfer to a cutting board. If desired, garnish with fresh basil. Cut into triangles or rectangles, and serve at once.

Warm Escarole Salad with Sausage & Potatoes

Following a spat with Antoine, Sylvie gives Emily a piece of her mind. This prompts Luc and Julien to whisk Emily away to the local bistro for lunch, gossip, and a warning not to step in more *merde*. This hearty salad makes a substantial lunch—just what you need to give you energy for a good fight—but it also makes a terrific dinner. Mildly bitter, sturdy escarole stands up to the big flavors that make up the salad, and a mustard vinaigrette adds the perfect bright note.

makes 4 servings

½ lb small Yukon gold potatoes, peeled or unpeeled

Fine sea salt and freshly ground black pepper

1 tablespoon unsalted butter

4 tablespoons extra-virgin olive oil, plus more if needed

1 clove garlic, chopped

4 baguette slices, cut into small cubes

4 smoked sausages, such as Toulouse or bratwurst

1 teaspoon red wine vinegar

1 teaspoon balsamic vinegar

2 teaspoons whole-grain mustard

1 large head escarole, pale yellow and green inner leaves only

¼ lb Gruyère, Comté, or cheddar cheese, cut into ½-inch cubes

In a saucepan, combine the potatoes with salted water to cover by 2 inches and bring to a boil over medium-high heat. Reduce the heat to medium and cook, stirring occasionally, until tender when pierced with a fork, about 20 minutes. Drain, let cool until they can be handled, and cut into ½-inch cubes.

In a large frying pan over medium-high heat, melt the butter with 1 tablespoon of the oil. When the butter foams, add the potatoes, sprinkle with ¼ teaspoon each salt and pepper, and cook, turning once, until golden brown on both sides, about 5 minutes on each side. Transfer to a bowl and keep warm. Reduce the heat to medium, add the garlic and bread cubes, and fry, turning occasionally, until golden, about 3 minutes, adding more oil if needed to prevent sticking. Transfer the croutons to a separate bowl.

Return the same pan to medium heat, add the sausages, and fry, turning several times to color the outside evenly, until cooked through, about 10 minutes. Transfer to a cutting board, let cool briefly, and cut into ½-inch-thick slices.

In a large bowl, whisk together the vinegars, mustard, and ¼ teaspoon each salt and pepper, then whisk in the remaining 3 tablespoons oil until the vinaigrette emulsifies. Add the escarole and toss to coat well. Add the potatoes, cheese, croutons, and sausage slices and toss gently. Transfer the salad to a platter or individual plates. Serve warm.

Beet & Mâche Salad with Citrus Dressing

Piles of freshly roasted beets are available at markets throughout Paris, which means this salad could be thrown together in a matter of minutes—a good thing when you have as many social engagements as Emily has. If you must roast them yourself, you can do it up to 3 days in advance, saving you time the day you serve the salad. Mâche, aka lamb's lettuce, is a mild, delicate winter salad green in France. Watercress can be substituted in a pinch.

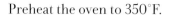

makes 4 servings

6 small beets or 3 large beets, about 1 lb total weight

4 tablespoons extra-virgin olive oil

1 tablespoon fresh lemon juice

2 tablespoons fresh orange juice

¼ teaspoon Dijon mustard

Fine sea salt and freshly ground black pepper

3 cups mâche or watercress (leaves and tender stems)

⅓ cup crumbled fresh goat cheese

2 tablespoons fresh minced flat-leaf parsley

Preheat the oven to 350°F.

If the beets still have their leafy tops, cut off the tops and reserve for another use. If using large beets, cut them in half. Place the beets in a roasting pan just large enough to accommodate them. Drizzle with 1½ tablespoons of the oil and toss to coat evenly. Cover the pan with aluminum foil and roast, turning the beets once or twice, until easily pierced with a fork, 45–60 minutes.

Let the beets cool until they can be handled, then slip off and discard the skins. Thinly slice the beets and set aside.

In a bowl, whisk together the remaining 2½ tablespoons oil, the lemon juice, orange juice, and mustard. Season with salt and pepper. Add the mâche and toss to coat evenly.

Divide the mâche among individual salad plates. Add the beets to the bowl and gently turn to coat in the remaining dressing. Divide the beets among the salads, tucking some under and some on top of the mâche. Sprinkle with the goat cheese, dividing it evenly. Garnish with the parsley and serve.

Croque Monsieur

Big, gooey, and rich, these hot ham-and-cheese sandwiches are so decadent they could almost be American. But the *croque monsieur* is decidedly French and decidedly comfort food. It's found in homes—think great brunch after a lot of French wine the night before—and in cafés and brasseries. For the best result, seek out high-quality brioche or *pain de mie* (sandwich bread) and *jambon de Paris*. To make a *croque madame*, top off the finished *croque monsieur* with a poached or fried egg.

makes 4 servings

8 thick slices brioche or sandwich bread

2 tablespoons unsalted butter, at room temperature

8 thin slices ham, preferably jambon de Paris

CHEESE SAUCE

2 tablespoons unsalted butter

⅓ cup all-purpose flour

1 teaspoon fine sea salt

Pinch of cayenne pepper

1½ cups whole milk

¾ cup shredded Gruyère cheese

Line up the bread slices on a work surface. Spread one side of each bread slice with the butter, dividing it evenly. Turn half of the slices buttered side down and lay 2 ham slices on the unbuttered side of each of the 4 bread slices. Cover with the remaining 4 bread slices, buttered side up.

To make the sauce, in a saucepan over medium heat, melt the butter. Remove the pan from the heat and whisk in the flour, salt, and cayenne. Return the pan to medium heat and gradually add the milk while whisking constantly to prevent lumps from forming. Reduce the heat to low and cook, stirring, until the sauce thickens, about 15 minutes. Stir in ¼ cup of the cheese until melted and remove from the heat. You should have about 1 cup sauce.

Preheat the broiler. Line a sheet pan with aluminum foil.

Warm a large frying pan over medium heat. Working in batches if necessary, place the sandwiches in the pan and cook, turning once, until both sides are golden, about 8 minutes total. Transfer the sandwiches to the prepared sheet pan.

Spoon about ¼ cup of the sauce over each sandwich. Top with the remaining ½ cup cheese, dividing it evenly among the sandwiches. Broil the sandwiches until the sauce bubbles and the cheese is golden, 4–5 minutes.

Transfer the sandwiches to warmed individual plates, cut each sandwich in half, and serve.

Plateau de Fromages

Emily's visit to the local open-air market highlights the gorgeous array of French cheeses available to her. Tasting and choosing a variety of French cheeses is the first step in creating *un plateau de fromages* worthy of Paris. Traditionally, the cheese course, which falls between the main course and dessert, includes cheeses made from different milks and of varying ages, textures, and moisture and fat content. Serve about 3 ounces cheese per person.

The Menu

Spring Selection
Saint-Nectaire (a medium-firm cow's milk cheese)
Montrachet (a mild goat's milk cheese)
Bleu de Bresse (a mild blue cow's milk cheese)
Strawberries, apricots, and baguette for serving

Summer Selection
Fourme d'Ambert (a semisoft, mild blue cow's milk cheese)
Banon (a mild goat's and/or cow's milk cheese)
Saint-André (a soft, triple crème cow's milk cheese)
Fresh Kadota or Mission figs, oven-roasted tomatoes, and
rosemary bread for serving

Autumn and Winter Selection
Young Crottin de Chavignol (a mild goat's milk cheese)
Reblochon (a semisoft cow's milk cheese)
Roquefort (a semihard blue sheep's milk cheese)
Chestnut honey, pears, quince paste, toasted walnuts, and
coarse country bread for serving

How to Build a Cheese Board

Although French desserts are world-famous, the final course of a traditional French meal is often a platter of carefully selected local cheeses. Here are some tips and suggested combinations to help you assemble an authentic French cheese course.

Selecting Cheeses

Focus on no more than three or four cheeses. One approach is to choose a firm aged cheese, a soft, young mild cheese and/or a goat's milk cheese, and a blue cheese. Try to aim for balance between aged, assertive cheeses and mild or creamy cheeses. Buy cheese freshly cut rather than prepackaged cheeses, and bring them to room temperature before serving (cold cheese lacks good texture and full flavor). Serve cheeses on a tray, board, or platter that can be easily passed from person to person. Provide small spreaders for soft cheeses and a cheese plane or sharp knife for harder cheeses.

It is perfectly fine to serve the cheeses with nothing more than a sliced baguette, but adding a few inventive accompaniments will elevate your selection from a simple cheese plate to a full-fledged course.

Choosing Accompaniments

Fruit is the most typical accompaniment, and grapes, pears, and apples will enhance nearly any cheese. Dried fruits, from apricots and prunes to figs, can offer a pleasant sweet counterpart, especially in cold weather. Walnuts, almonds, and hazelnuts, served in the shell with a nutcracker and pick or shelled and lightly toasted, are also customary accompaniments.

Finally, chunky, sweetened conserves or preserves, such as apricot, peach, or sour cherry, make interesting matches with cheeses, especially if served with rustic bread. A drizzle of honey and sweet-spicy quince paste are also excellent additions.

Pairing Wine

Pour wine to match the cheese, in general, a sweeter fortified wine, such as a port, is traditional with pungent cheeses, such as Roquefort. Lighter, fresher cheeses go best with white wine. More robust cheeses, especially hard cheeses, go well with reds.

Plateau de Fruits de Mer

An extravagant assortment of oysters, shrimp, crab, lobster, and clams, this seafood platter is worthy of a special occasion. The seafood is excellent dipped into a classic mignonette, but you can take this *plateau* up a notch by also serving warm melted butter alongside. Set out a loaf of crusty bread and wash it all down with a crisp French white wine.

makes 6 servings

Shellfish, such as crab, lobster, shrimp, oysters, and clams

Crushed ice, for serving

Mignonette Sauce (page 210)

2 lemons, cut into wedges

Select the shellfish that appeals to you. For example, for six servings, you might purchase 1 lobster, 1 crab, 2 lb shrimp in the shell, 18–24 oysters, and 12–18 littleneck clams.

You can purchase live crab and lobster and cook them or buy them already cooked.

Shuck the oysters (see Oysters with Mignonette Sauce, page 64), and clams and serve them on the half shell, or serve the clams with the shells open but hinges intact. Cover a large serving platter with the ice and arrange the shellfish on it.

Accompany with the sauce, chilled or at room temperature, and with the lemon wedges.

Oysters with Mignonette Sauce

Mindy invites Emily to a party of French-speaking Parisians at her apartment, and Emily soon retreats to the terrace for some air. A cute guy named Fabien follows her, and they are soon walking on a cobblestoned street along the Seine to a charming riverside wine and raw seafood bar. It should be a romantic moment, but Fabien offends Emily, and she runs off. A chilled glass of white wine or Champagne is the perfect accompaniment to raw oysters with mignonette, a tangy vinegar and shallot sauce. Just leave the rude French guy at the party.

makes 6–8 servings

Mignonette Sauce (page 210)

24 small-to-medium oysters in the shell

Crushed ice, for serving

Make the sauce and refrigerate as directed.

Scrub and rinse the oysters well under cold running water. Cover a large serving tray with crushed ice. Working with 1 oyster at a time, use a thick folded cloth to hold the oyster, with the flat top shell facing up, in your nondominant hand. Using an oyster knife in your dominant hand, insert the tip between the shells near the hinge (where the shells taper). Twist the knife with a bit of strength to break the hinge. Run the knife along the inside surface of the top shell to loosen the oyster from it. Lift off and discard the top shell. Run the knife along the inside surface of the bottom shell to sever the muscle that attaches the oyster to the shell, then nest the oyster in its bottom shell in the ice, being careful not to tip the shell and lose the liquor. Repeat with the remaining oysters.

Place the bowl of sauce on the serving tray with the oysters and serve.

Moules Frites

In this Parisian classic, mussels are briefly simmered in white wine, butter, and shallots, creating an aromatic broth perfect for dunking hot, crispy fries. Choose fresh mussels with tightly closed shells and cook them within a day of purchase. To store until cooking, refrigerate in a deep bowl covered with a damp kitchen towel. No time to make the *frites?* Serve the mussels with thick slices of crusty bread.

makes 6 first-course servings or 2 main-course servings

Pomme Frites (page 211)

2 cups dry white wine

4 shallots, minced

6 tablespoons unsalted butter

4 tablespoons finely chopped fresh flat-leaf parsley leaves

1 small bay leaf

Freshly ground black pepper

4 lb cultivated mussels, scrubbed and errant beards removed

Prepare the frites as directed, frying once, up to 2 hours in advance.

In a large stockpot over medium-high heat, combine the wine, shallots, butter, 2 tablespoons of the parsley, the bay leaf, and a couple of grinds of pepper. Bring to a simmer and cook, uncovered, until the broth is aromatic, 4–5 minutes.

While the stock simmers, reheat the oil for the frites to 370°F. Fry the potatoes in batches the second time as directed, then drain and season generously with salt.

Add the mussels to the stockpot, discarding any that do not close to the touch. Cover the pot tightly and steam the mussels, shaking the pot occasionally so they cook evenly, until they open, about 5 minutes.

To serve, using a slotted spoon, transfer the mussels to large soup bowls, checking carefully and discarding any that failed to open. Ladle some of the broth over each serving and sprinkle with the remaining 2 tablespoons parsley. Serve at once, with the frites alongside.

Sole Meunière with Potato Purée

This dish of pan-seared sole fillets dressed with a sauce of browned butter, lemon, and capers comes together quickly, making it the ideal meal for a girl on the go like Emily. It also appealed to an earlier American in Paris. According to Julia Child's memoir *My Life in France*, it is the dish that made her "fall in love with French cuisine." Make the potatoes first, then cover and keep them warm for serving.

makes 4 servings

POTATO PURÉE

4 boiling potatoes, such as Yukon gold, about 2½ lb total weight, peeled and cut into 2-inch chunks

Fine sea salt and freshly ground black pepper

2 tablespoons unsalted butter, at room temperature

½ cup whole milk, warmed

¼–½ cup heavy cream, warmed

SOLE MEUNIÈRE

4 sole fillets, preferably Dover sole, each about 6 oz

2 tablespoons extra-virgin olive oil

Fine sea salt and freshly ground black pepper

¼ cup all-purpose flour

6 tablespoons unsalted butter

Juice of 1 lemon

2 tablespoons capers

2 tablespoons finely chopped fresh flat-leaf parsley leaves

Lemon wedges for garnish

To make the potato purée, in a saucepan, combine the potatoes with salted water to cover by 2 inches and bring to a boil over medium-high heat. Reduce the heat to medium and cook, stirring occasionally, until tender when pierced with a fork, about 20 minutes. Drain the potatoes into a colander, then pass them through a ricer or food mill back into the hot pan. (Alternatively, return them to the hot pan and mash with a potato masher.) Add 2 teaspoons salt, ½ teaspoon pepper, butter, and ¼ cup of the milk and beat with a fork until fully incorporated. While continuing to beat vigorously, gradually pour in the remaining ¼ cup milk and as much of the cream as needed to make a fluffy, smooth consistency. Taste and adjust the seasoning with salt and pepper. Cover to keep warm and set aside.

To make the sole meunière, rinse the sole fillets and pat dry with paper towels. Rub the fillets with the oil, ½ teaspoon salt, and ¼ teaspoon pepper. Spread the flour on a plate. One at a time, lightly coat the fillets on both sides with the flour, shaking off the excess.

In a large frying pan over medium-high heat, melt 3 tablespoons of the butter. When the butter foams, reduce the heat to medium, add the fish fillets, and fry, turning once, until lightly golden on both sides and opaque in the center when prodded with a knife tip, 8–10 minutes total. Transfer to a warmed serving platter.

With the pan still over medium-high heat, melt the remaining 3 tablespoons butter, then scrape the pan bottom with a wooden spoon to dislodge any browned bits. Heat the butter until it begins to brown, about 2 minutes, then stir in the lemon juice and capers.

Spoon the sauce over the the fish, garnish each with a lemon wedge and serve at once with the potato purée.

Choucroute Alsacienne

This dish became popular in Paris in the 1870s, when a flood of emigrants from Alsace opened *brasseries alsaciennes* in the city, most of which doubled as breweries. The beer making is gone from these traditional spots, but Alsatian sauerkraut, or *choucroute*, still shows up regularly on brasserie menus. This version is chock-full of sausage, ham hock, bacon, and potatoes, but you can simplify it by leaving any of the meats out.

makes 6–8 servings

3 lb raw or cooked sauerkraut

1 clove garlic, minced

10 juniper berries

1 bay leaf

2 whole cloves

6 black peppercorns

¼ cup rendered duck or goose fat or olive oil

1 large yellow onion, minced

4 smoked ham hocks, about 2 lb total weight

2 cups dry Riesling, Sylvaner, or other dry white wine

½ teaspoon freshly ground black pepper

½ lb slab bacon, in one piece

¼ lb skinless pork belly, in one piece (optional)

3 lb small Yukon gold potatoes, peeled

6 smoked pork or chicken sausages

Preheat the oven to 325°F.

If using raw sauerkraut, soak the sauerkraut in a large bowl of cold water for 15 minutes. Taste the sauerkraut and continued to soak if it is too salty. Drain the raw or cooked sauerkraut, pile it onto a kitchen towel, gather up the towel ends, and wring out any excess water. Transfer the sauerkraut to a bowl and, using a fork, fluff to remove any clumps.

Cut a small square of cheesecloth. Place the garlic, juniper berries, bay leaf, cloves, and peppercorns in the center, bring the corners together, and tie securely with kitchen twine.

In a Dutch oven or other heavy ovenproof pot over medium heat, warm the fat until melted. Add the onion and cook slowly, reducing the heat if necessary, until translucent but not browned, about 5 minutes. Add half of the sauerkraut, the spice bundle, and the ham hocks, and top with the remaining sauerkraut. Add the wine, ground pepper, and water almost to cover and bring to a boil.

Cover, transfer to the oven, and cook for 1 hour. Remove from the oven, stir, and add the bacon and the pork belly, if using. Re-cover and cook for 1 hour longer. Remove from the oven, stir, and place the potatoes on top. Re-cover and cook until the potatoes are tender when pierced with a fork, about 30 minutes longer.

Meanwhile, in a large frying pan over medium heat, cook the sausage, turning as needed, until browned all over, about 10 minutes. Remove from the heat and keep warm.

Remove the sauerkraut mixture from the oven. Scoop out the potatoes, ham hocks, bacon, and pork belly (if using) and keep warm. Remove and discard the spice bundle. Drain the sauerkraut into a colander and turn once or twice. Transfer to a warmed, deep platter, mounding it in the center, and top with the ham hocks and sausages. Cut the bacon and pork belly (if using) into slices and arrange the slices on the sauerkraut. Surround the sauerkraut with the potatoes. Serve at once.

Pierre's Cracked Crème Brûlée

At the American Friends of the Louvre auction, a model fails to appear and Emily ends up wearing Pierre Cadault's dress. After the avant-garde designers of Grey Space submit the winning bid for Pierre's creation, they spray the dress—and Emily—with paint, shocking the crowd. Pierre promptly retreats to his home, where Emily finds him the next day on his bed cracking crème brûlées, a sound he finds satisfying. These crème brûlées yield that same "satisfying" sound as you crack the sugary crust with the back of a spoon, giving way to a smooth, rich custard.

makes 6 servings

3 cups heavy cream

½ vanilla bean, split lengthwise, or 1 teaspoon pure vanilla extract

8 large egg yolks

⅓ cup granulated sugar

⅓ cup turbinado sugar

Preheat the oven to 300°F. Place six ¾-cup ramekins in a shallow roasting pan.

Pour the cream into a saucepan. If using the vanilla bean, using the tip of a knife, scrape the seeds of the bean into the cream, then add the pod to the cream. Bring the cream to a gentle boil over medium heat. Remove from the heat, cover, and let steep for 15–30 minutes. Remove and discard the pod. If using vanilla extract, reserve for adding later.

Return the cream to medium heat and bring almost to a boil. Remove from the heat. In a large bowl, whisk together the egg yolks and the granulated sugar just until blended. While whisking constantly, slowly whisk in the hot cream mixture. Pour the mixture into the saucepan, set over medium-low heat, and cook, stirring constantly, until the custard is thick enough to coat the back of a spoon, about 3 minutes. Do not let it boil. Remove from the heat. If using vanilla extract, stir it into the custard, mixing well.

Pour the custard through a fine-mesh sieve into a container with a spout, then pour into the ramekins, dividing it evenly. Transfer the roasting pan to the center oven rack and pour hot water into the pan to come halfway up the sides of the ramekins. Bake the custards until set but the centers still jiggle slightly when the ramekins are gently shaken, about 40 minutes.

Carefully remove the roasting pan from the oven and let the custards cool in the water bath until the ramekins are cool enough to handle. Lift out the ramekins, cover each ramekin with plastic wrap, and refrigerate until well chilled, at least 3 hours or up to overnight.

Sprinkle custards with turbinado sugar. Using a kitchen torch, caramelize the sugar, slowly and steadily moving it over the sugar until it melts. Lets sit for a few minutes to set the caramel, then serve.

Îles Flottantes

These little, fluffy meringue islands floating in a sea of crème anglaise and drizzled with caramel are old-fashioned, but they still appear on many Parisian menus. And it's a good thing too, because this treat is timeless. If you like, garnish with toasted sliced almonds. The crème anglaise can be made in advance, with everything else *à la minute*.

makes 8 servings

CRÈME ANGLAISE

2 cups whole milk

2 large whole eggs plus 2 large egg yolks

¼ cup sugar

⅛ teaspoon fine sea salt

1 teaspoon pure vanilla extract

MERINGUES

4 egg whites, at room temperature

½ cup sugar

¼ teaspoon pure vanilla extract

Caramel syrup (page 214)

To make the crème anglaise, pour the milk into a saucepan and heat over medium heat until small bubbles appear along the pan edge and steam begins to rise from the milk. Meanwhile, in a heatproof bowl, whisk together the whole eggs and egg yolks until blended, then whisk in the sugar, salt, and vanilla until the sugar dissolves. While whisking constantly, slowly drizzle the hot milk into egg mixture.

Place the bowl on top of a saucepan over (not touching) simmering water and heat, stirring constantly, until the sauce is thick enough to coat the back of a spoon, about 5 minutes. Remove from heat, pour through a fine-mesh sieve into a small saucepan, and cover to keep warm. (The sauce can be transferred to an airtight container and refrigerated for up to 5 days. Reheat before serving.)

To make the meringues, using an electric mixer on medium speed, beat the egg whites until soft peaks form. Add the sugar and beat on medium speed until stiff peaks form. Beat in the vanilla.

Line a plate with paper towels. Fill a wide saucepan to within 1 inch of the top with water. Place the pan over medium-high heat and bring the water to just below a simmer, adjusting the heat as needed. Working in batches and using 2 soup spoons, scoop a mound of meringue onto a spoon, then push it off into the water with the second spoon, forming a rough oval. Repeat until the pan is about one-third full, then poach, carefully flipping each meringue once, for 3–4 minutes. Turn off the heat and continue to cook until the whites are firm, 5–8 minutes longer. Using a slotted spoon or wire skimmer, transfer the meringues to the paper towels to drain. Repeat with the remaining meringue. You should have 16 meringues.

To serve, rewarm the crème anglaise over low heat. Divide it among 8 shallow bowls. Using an offset spatula, slide 2 meringues into each bowl. Drizzle the meringues with the caramel syrup and serve at once.

LE RESTAURANT

Country-Style Pâté
with Cornichons

A beautiful sliced pâté en croute served with tangy cornichons makes an appearance at the dinner Emily arranges for Randy Zimmer, whom she hopes to recruit as a client for Savoir. Although this country-style pâté lacks a pastry crust, it would make a memorable first course for a special dinner or a satisfying main course paired with a tangle of salad greens for a very Parisian lunch. You may need to order the pork liver, fatback, and caul fat from your butcher in advance. Curing salt can be purchased online.

makes 12–14 servings

½ lb pork fatback, cut
into ½-inch cubes

2 lb boneless pork shoulder,
cut into 1-inch cubes

Coarse sea salt and freshly
ground black pepper

¼ teaspoon curing salt

½ bay leaf, crumbled

2 allspice berries, finely crushed

2 juniper berries, finely crushed

¼ teaspoon yellow mustard seeds

¼ teaspoon sweet Spanish paprika

Pinch of freshly grated nutmeg

¼ cup brandy

¼ lb fresh pork liver

2 cups whole milk, plus more as needed

3 cups heavy cream

¼ cup chicken broth

2 tablespoons fresh bread crumbs

1 piece caul fat, about 16 inches square,
well rinsed under cold running water

Cornichons, Crostini (page 210), and
whole-grain mustard, for serving

In a large bowl, combine the fatback, pork shoulder, 1 tablespoon sea salt, ½ teaspoon pepper, curing salt, bay leaf, allspice and juniper berries, mustard seeds, paprika, nutmeg, and brandy. Using your hands, mix well. In a medium bowl, combine the liver and milk, adding more milk if needed to cover the liver. Cover both bowls and refrigerate overnight.

Drain the liver and discard the milk. Rinse the liver thoroughly under running cold water and pat dry with paper towels. Cut the liver into 1-inch cubes, add to the pork mixture, and mix well. Transfer the pork mixture to a food processor and pulse until finely chopped. Return the mixture to the large bowl.

Rinse and dry the medium bowl, then add the cream, broth, and bread crumbs and stir well. Add the cream mixture to the ground meat mixture and mix well with your hands. Transfer the new mixture to the food processor and pulse until well mixed, 1–2 minutes. The mixture will be loose and wet.

Preheat the oven to 300°F. Line a 2-quart pâté mold or loaf pan with the caul fat, allowing it to drape over the ends and sides.

Tightly pack the meat mixture into the prepared mold. Tap the mold on a work surface several times to eliminate any air pockets. Fold the exposed caul fat over the top of the mold to enclose the meat mixture completely.

continued on next page

continued from page 83

Cover the mold and place it in a deep baking dish. Pour boiling water into the baking dish to come halfway up the sides of the mold. Bake the pâté until an instant-read thermometer inserted into the center registers 145°F, about 1½ hours. As the pâté bakes, check the water level from time to time and add more boiling if needed to maintain the original level.

Transfer the mold, still covered, to a wire rack. Top with a weight, such as a brick wrapped in aluminum foil, and let cool to room temperature. Remove the weight, then refrigerate for at least 2 days before serving.

To serve, uncover the mold and slide a knife along the entire edge of the pâté to loosen it. Gently warm the bottom of the mold in warm water for a few seconds, then invert a flat plate on top of the mold, invert the plate and mold together, and lift off the mold. Cut the pâté into slices about ½ inch thick and serve with the cornichons, crostini, and mustard.

Beef Tartare with Crostini

During an important work dinner with hotelier Randy Zimmer at Les Deux Compères, perfumer Antoine and Emily's boss, Sylvie, drop plenty of sexual innuendos. By the end of the dinner, Randy agrees to work with Antoine to create a signature scent for his hotel. Gabriel's sexy *tartare de veau* is later confirmed to have "helped seal the deal." The success of this vintage starter depends on securing impeccably fresh, good-quality raw beef.

makes 25 canapes

Crostini (page 210)

BEEF TARTARE

½ lb filet mignon, trimmed of all fat and gristle

¼ cup minced white onion

¼ cup capers, rinsed and finely chopped

1 tablespoon fresh lime juice

1 teaspoon Worcestershire sauce

1 teaspoon extra-virgin olive oil

Dash of Tabasco or other hot-pepper sauce

2 tablespoons finely chopped fresh flat-leaf parsley, for garnish

Make the crostini as directed up to one day in advance.

To make the beef tartare, place the filet mignon in the freezer for 20 minutes to firm it up. In a large bowl, combine the onion, capers, lime juice, Worcestershire sauce, oil, and Tabasco sauce. Mix well, cover, and refrigerate.

On a very clean cutting board, cut the beef into ¼-inch dice. Transfer the beef to a food processor and pulse briefly 6–8 times, until the beef is ground but not pulverized. Transfer the beef to the bowl containing the onion mixture and, using a fork, mix together quickly but thoroughly.

Working quickly so the beef mixture remains chilled, top each crostini with a large spoonful of the beef mixture. Sprinkle the beef with the parsley and serve right away.

Soufflé au Fromage

Light and airy as a cloud, soufflés have a reputation for being difficult to make. But just a few tips will have you turning out a towering soufflé to rival that of any French chef. First, when beating the egg whites, make sure the bowl, beaters, and whites are free of drops of egg yolk or other fat or grease that can inhibit volume. Second, to keep the air in the just-whipped whites, use a rubber spatula and gentle, sweeping motions to fold them into the soufflé base. Finally, remember, a soufflé waits for no one, so be ready to sit down to eat the moment it comes out of the oven—and immediately after a shot for Instagram.

makes 4 servings

3 tablespoons unsalted butter, plus more for the soufflé dish

1 cup plus 2 tablespoons shredded Gruyère or Comté cheese

3 tablespoons all-purpose flour

1 cup whole milk

4 large egg yolks

1 teaspoon Dijon mustard

Fine sea salt and ground white pepper

Pinch of freshly grated nutmeg

5 large egg whites

Pinch of cream of tartar

1 tablespoon dried bread crumbs

Preheat the oven to 375°F. Butter the bottom and sides of a 6-cup soufflé dish and then coat the bottom and sides evenly with 1 tablespoon of the cheese.

In a saucepan over medium heat, melt the butter. Add the flour and stir constantly with a whisk for 1 minute. Continue to cook, stirring often, until the mixture is bubbling but still white, about 2 minutes longer. While whisking constantly, slowly add the milk. Bring to a simmer and continue to whisk until the sauce is thick and smooth, about 2 minutes longer. Remove from the heat and let cool for 10 minutes.

Whisk the egg yolks into the cooled milk mixture until smooth. Add the mustard, $\frac{1}{2}$ teaspoon salt, a pinch of pepper, and the nutmeg and whisk until blended.

In a bowl, using an electric mixer on medium speed, whip together the egg whites, cream of tartar, and a pinch of salt until stiff peaks form.

Using a rubber spatula, gently fold half of the egg whites into the milk mixture to lighten it. Gently stir in 1 cup of the cheese and then fold in the remaining egg whites just until no white streaks remain. Scoop the egg mixture into the prepared dish and sprinkle with the remaining 1 tablespoon cheese and the bread crumbs.

Bake the soufflé until puffed and the top is browned, 30–35 minutes. Serve at once.

Plateau de Charcuteries

Getting together with girlfriends for dinner is always fun, especially if it involves a big array of charcuterie selections and plenty of wine—and it's at Les Deux Compères. While eating with Mindy and Camille, Emily invites them to the Fourtier launch party, but neither of them can make it. Luckily for Emily, Gabriel is available. A charcuterie board laden with assorted cured meats, accompaniments like olives and cornichons, and a crusty baguette is perfect for sharing among friends—and between lovers.

The Menu

Meats

Terrine (pâté (see below) made of meat, fish, or vegetables)

Jambon Blanc (ham that has been brined and then boiled and is served very thinly sliced)

Saucisson (sausage of pork or mixed meats that is air-dried and served very thinly sliced)

Rillettes (rich spread of shredded meat, such as pork, duck, goose, or, more rarely, chicken or turkey)

Mousse (smooth, spreadable mixture made from a variety of meats, often chicken or pork liver)

Pâté (a mixture of chopped and ground meats of pork, veal, and/or rabbit)

Accompaniments

Niçoise or Picholine olives

Cornichons

Butter

Baguette slices, Crostini (page 210), or crackers

Cheeses (page 58)

Toasted marcona almonds, pistachios, or pecans

Fresh fruits such as figs, grapes, apple slices, or cherries

Whole-grain mustard, chutney, or fig jam

Prepare the Platter

After you have made your charcuterie selections, arrange them on a large platter or wooden serving board. Rillettes and some pâtés, such as chicken or pork liver mousse, are typically served in small bowls, as are olives and butter. Other meats, such as country-style pâtés and sausages, are served in slices, as are breads. Prepare the platter just before you are ready to serve so the meat doesn't sit out too long and the bread remains fresh.

Choose Your Meats

When making selections for a charcuterie platter, include meats that have different textures. For example, rillettes are a creamy spread, thinly sliced saucisson adds a chewy component, and a pâté or terrine can range in texture from silky smooth to coarse. The menu at left suggests some different items to consider.

Add the Accoutrements

Always offer accompaniments to complement the charcuterie, such as brined or oil-cured olives, cornichons, toasted nuts, mustard, chutney, and bread. Butter is rarely offered with bread in France but always appears when charcuterie is served.

Gabriel's Omelette aux Fines Herbes

Who could resist a cute French chef teaching you how to cook? Not Emily. "Oh, my God! I feel like I've never had an omelet before. This was amazing." With just a flick of the wrist and a few tips, you can make your own French-style omelet. Be sure to use a well-seasoned pan, just as Gabriel did—"That's the secret to our omelets. We never clean. We let things season."

makes 2 servings

4 large eggs

1 tablespoon minced fresh chives, tarragon, flat-leaf parsley, and chervil, in equal parts, or fresh herb mixture of choice

Fine sea salt

2 tablespoons unsalted butter

In a bowl, whisk together the eggs, half of the herb mixture, and a pinch of salt.

Warm a 7- or 8-inch nonstick frying pan over medium-low heat. Add 1 tablespoon of the butter, tilting the pan as it melts to distribute the butter evenly over the pan bottom. Pour half of the eggs into the pan.

Let the eggs heat slightly, then use a rubber spatula to stir the eggs vigorously until creamy but very softly scrambled. Make sure the eggs are not sticking to the bottom of the pan. If they are, gently loosen them with the spatula. Spread the eggs in an even layer. Remove the pan from the heat and, lifting the handle, tilt the pan away from you, and then gently roll the portion of the omelet nearest you over itself. Now, gently ease the omelet to the far edge of the pan and carefully fold the overhang over the top, overlapping the first fold. The omelet should have an oval shape and not be browned.

Slide the omelet onto a serving plate and top with half of the remaining herb mixture. Serve at once. Repeat to make the second omelet with the remaining eggs, first wiping out the pan and then melting the butter before proceeding.

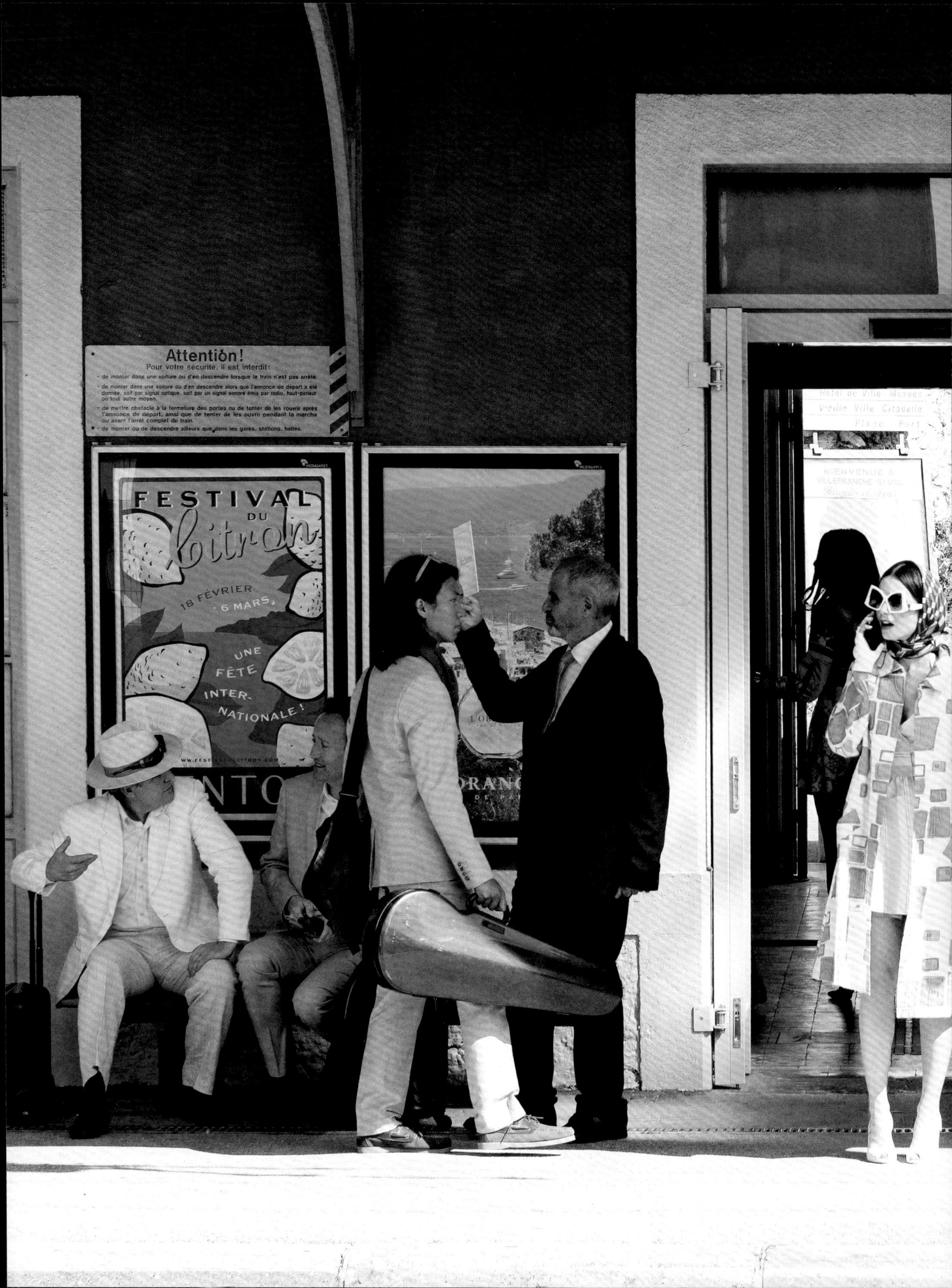

FESTIVAL DU citron

18 FÉVRIER - 6 MARS

UNE FÊTE INTER- NATIONALE!

WW.FESTIVALDUCITRON.COM

Gabriel's Coq au Vin

Emily visits Camille's family's château and meets Gérard, Camille's father, who is lying naked by the pool. Gérard asks Emily if she has tasted Gabriel's *coq au vin*, telling her, "When it hit my lips, I was ready to propose to him!" *Coq au vin*, literally "rooster with wine," originated as a way to make an old bird tender, but nowadays this classic dish is most often made with a cut-up young whole chicken. This simplified version uses bone-in chicken thighs to keep things easy. Serve it with mashed or roasted potatoes and maybe someone will want to propose to you.

makes 6 servings

5 tablespoons all-purpose flour

Fine sea salt and freshly ground black pepper

5 lb skinless, bone-in chicken thighs

2 tablespoons unsalted butter, at room temperature

10 shallots, roughly chopped

¼ lb thick-cut bacon slices, cut into ½-inch pieces

1 bottle (750 ml) dry red wine

9 oz button mushrooms, brushed clean and sliced

2 fresh thyme sprigs

1 bay leaf

Chopped fresh flat-leaf parsley, for garnish

Preheat the oven to 325°F. Put 4 tablespoons of the flour into a shallow bowl and season with salt and pepper. Dust the chicken thighs with the seasoned flour, coating them evenly and tapping off the excess.

In a large Dutch oven or other heavy ovenproof pot over medium heat, melt 1 tablespoon of the butter. Add the shallots and cook, stirring, until beginning to soften, about 3 minutes. Add the bacon and continue to cook, stirring, until the shallots are caramelized and the bacon is crisp, about 5 minutes. Using a slotted spoon, transfer the shallots and bacon to a plate.

Raise the heat to medium-high. Working in batches to avoid crowding, add the chicken thighs to the fat remaining in the pot and cook, turning once, until golden brown on both sides, 5–8 minutes on each side. As each batch is ready, transfer it to a plate. When all the chicken is browned, return the shallots and bacon to the pot. Pour in the wine, bring to a simmer, and deglaze the pot, scraping the pot bottom with a wooden spoon to dislodge any browned bits. Add the chicken pieces, mushrooms, thyme, and bay leaf, return to a simmer, and cook for 10 minutes, then cover, transfer to the oven, and cook until the chicken is so tender it is nearly falling from the bone, about 1 hour.

Remove the pot from the oven and, using a slotted spoon, transfer the chicken to a plate. Cover the chicken with aluminum foil to keep warm. Remove and discard the thyme sprigs and bay leaf.

In a small bowl, using a fork, work together the remaining 1 tablespoon each flour and butter to form a uniform paste. Place the pot on the stove top and bring to a boil over medium heat. Gradually whisk in the butter mixture until completely dissolved. Adjust the heat to maintain a simmer and simmer until the liquid thickens, about 15 minutes.

Return the chicken to the pot and rewarm in the sauce for a few minutes, then serve, garnished with parsley.

Ratatouille

"The entire city looks like [the movie] *Ratatouille*," exclaims Emily to her then-boyfriend Doug as she stands on a bridge over the Seine, the lights of Paris sparkling against the evening sky. Although she is clearly not referring to this mix of deep-purple eggplants, summer squash, sweet red peppers, ripe tomatoes, and basil, there are few more quintessential French dishes than this one.

makes 4 servings

3 tablespoons olive oil

1 yellow onion, chopped

1 Italian eggplant, about ½ lb, peeled and cut into 1-inch cubes

1 red bell pepper, seeded and chopped

2 cloves garlic, minced

4 large tomatoes, about 3 lb total weight, peeled and coarsely chopped

1 zucchini, trimmed and chopped

1 fresh rosemary sprig

1 fresh thyme sprig

Fine sea salt and freshly ground black pepper

¼ cup chopped fresh basil leaves

In a large, heavy pot over medium heat, warm 2 tablespoons of the oil. Add the onion and cook, stirring occasionally, until softened, about 5 minutes. Add the eggplant, bell pepper, and garlic and cook, stirring occasionally, until the vegetables have softened, about 5 minutes. Add the remaining 1 tablespoon oil, the tomatoes, zucchini, rosemary, and thyme and season with salt and pepper. Cook, stirring occasionally, until the tomatoes begin to break down, about 3 minutes.

Cover, reduce the heat to low, and cook, stirring occasionally, until the vegetables are soft and somewhat blended together, about 15 minutes. Stir in the basil and remove from the heat.

Remove and discard the rosemary and thyme sprigs, then season with salt and pepper and serve, garnished with the basil.

Bouillabaisse

A bowl of this seafood stew will transport you to the coastal city of Marseille. The tomato base is flavored with leeks, fennel, and orange zest. Start with firm white fish fillets and then add your favorite shellfish, such as the shrimp and mussels or clams or scallops. To save time, the toasts are spread with an easy-to-make version of *rouille*, which calls for just mayonnaise, red pepper, and garlic.

makes 6 servings

BOUILLABAISSE

¼ cup olive oil

1 yellow onion, finely chopped

2 leeks, white part only, chopped

1 long orange zest strip

2 tomatoes, peeled and chopped

1 small fennel bulb, trimmed, cored, and thinly sliced, with fronds reserved for garnish

2 cloves garlic, crushed

2 fresh thyme sprigs

1 bay leaf

Fine sea salt and freshly ground black pepper

2 cups dry white wine

1 cup cold water

5 boiling potatoes, peeled and cut into ½-inch slices

¼ teaspoon saffron threads

2 lb firm, white-fleshed fish fillets, such as halibut or cod, cut into 1½-inch chunks

1 lb medium shrimp, peeled and deveined, or squid, cleaned and cut into rings

1 lb mussels, scrubbed and errant beards removed

3 tablespoons chopped flat-leaf parsley

TOASTS

½ cup mayonnaise

¼ cup minced roasted red bell pepper

1 clove garlic, minced

6 slices coarse country bread, toasted and rubbed with 1 clove garlic

To make the bouillabaisse, in a large Dutch oven or other heavy pot over medium-high-heat, warm the oil. Add the onion and leeks and cook, stirring often, until translucent, 2–3 minutes. Stir in the orange zest strip, tomatoes, fennel, garlic, thyme, and bay leaf and season with ½ teaspoon each salt and pepper. Add the wine, water, and potatoes and bring to a boil. Reduce the heat to low, cover, and simmer until the potatoes are nearly tender, about 25 minutes.

Raise the heat to medium-high and bring to a rolling boil. Stir in the saffron. Place the fish on top of the stew, add boiling water as needed just to cover, and boil until the fish is half-cooked, about 5 minutes. Add the shrimp and mussels, discarding any mussels that fail to close to the touch, and then add boiling water as needed just to cover and boil just until the shrimp are pink and the mussels open, 3–4 minutes. Remove from the heat and discard any unopened mussels.

Just before the stew is ready, make the toasts. In a small bowl, stir together the mayonnaise, bell pepper, and garlic. Place a slice of toasted bread in the bottom of each individual serving bowl and top each slice with a dollop of the mayonnaise mixture.

Using a slotted spoon, divide the seafood and potatoes evenly among the bowls. Ladle the broth over the top, sprinkle with the parsley, and serve right away. Pass the remaining mayonnaise mixture at the table for diners to stir into their stew as desired.

Bourride

Richly flavored *bourride*, a fish stew thickened with garlicky aioli, is one of the culinary treasures of coastal Provence. A quick fish stock flavored with carrots, fennel, celery, and herbs forms the base of the dish. Choose whatever firm, white-fleshed fish looks best at the market. You can make the aioli with your favorite recipe, but using purchased aioli keeps this dish quick and easy.

makes 6 servings

1½ lb heads, tails, backbones, and other trimmings from nonoily fish

2 carrots, quartered crosswise

1 yellow onion, quartered

1 fennel bulb, trimmed and quartered

3 cloves garlic

1 celery rib, quartered

4 fresh flat-leaf parsley sprigs

3 fresh thyme sprigs

1 bay leaf

2-inch piece dried orange peel

1 teaspoon fine sea salt

8 cups water

2 cups dry white wine

2 lb firm, white-fleshed fish fillets, such as monkfish or haddock, cut into 1-inch chunks

6 slices day-old coarse country bread, each about 1 inch thick

1 cup purchased aioli

6 egg yolks

Chopped fresh flat-leaf parsley

In a large pot over medium-high heat, combine the fish trimmings, carrots, onion, fennel, garlic, celery, parsley and thyme sprigs, bay leaf, orange peel, salt, and water. Bring to a boil, skimming off any foam that forms on the surface. Reduce the heat to low and simmer for 15 minutes. Add the wine, raise the heat to high, and bring to a boil. Reduce the heat to low and simmer for 15 minutes longer. Using a slotted spoon or skimmer, remove and discard the solids. Line a fine-mesh sieve with several layers of cheesecloth and strain the stock into a large clean saucepan. You should have about 6 cups.

Place the saucepan over medium heat and bring the stock to a simmer. Add the fish and cook just until opaque, about 5 minutes. Using a slotted spoon, transfer the fish to a platter and cover loosely with aluminum foil to keep warm.

Place a bread slice in the bottom of each individual serving bowl. Ladle just enough of the hot stock into each bowl for the bread to absorb.

In a large, heatproof bowl, whisk together ½ cup of the aioli and the egg yolks until well blended. While whisking constantly, add the remaining stock in a slow, steady stream to the yolk mixture. Pour the mixture into a clean saucepan and place over very low heat. Cook, stirring gently and being very careful not to let the mixture boil, until thickened to the consistency of light cream, 6–7 minutes.

Divide the fish evenly among the bowls, arranging it on top of the bread. Ladle the creamy stock over the top and garnish with the chopped parsley. Serve at once. Pass the remaining ½ cup aioli at the table for diners to add to their stew as desired.

Roast Salmon with French Lentils

Roast salmon on a bed of French green lentils flavored with lemon and herbs is a great choice for a long, leisurely lunch away from work. The most celebrated green lentils of France are cultivated around the town of Le Puy-en-Velay in the Haute-Loire. The tiny, deep-green legumes mottled with blue keep their shape and subtle flavor when cooked, making them a favorite for lentil salads and side dishes.

makes 6 servings

1 cup French green lentils, preferably Le Puy, picked over, rinsed, and drained

4 cups chicken broth

4 tablespoons olive oil

1 red onion, finely chopped

1 celery rib, finely chopped

1 carrot, peeled and finely chopped

1 small red bell pepper, seeded and finely chopped

3 tablespoons fresh lemon juice

2 tablespoons finely chopped fresh flat-leaf parsley, plus more for garnish

2 tablespoons finely chopped basil, plus more for garnish

Fine sea salt and freshly ground black pepper

6 skinless salmon fillets, each about 6 oz

In a saucepan over medium-high heat, combine the lentils and 3½ cups of the broth and bring to a boil. Reduce the heat to medium-low, cover, and simmer until the lentils are tender but not mushy, about 30 minutes. Drain and set aside. Just before the lentils are ready, preheat the oven to 450°F.

In a frying pan over medium heat, warm 3 tablespoons of the oil. Add the onion and cook, stirring occasionally, until softened, 5–7 minutes. Add the celery and carrot and cook, stirring occasionally, until slightly softened, about 2 minutes. Add the bell pepper and cook, stirring, until softened, about 2 minutes. Add the lentils to the pan and cook over medium heat, stirring occasionally, for about 2 minutes to blend the flavors. Stir in the lemon juice, the remaining 1 tablespoon oil, and the chopped parsley and basil and season with salt and pepper. Remove from the heat.

Transfer 1 cup of the lentil mixture to a blender or food processor and process until puréed, adding just enough of the remaining ½ cup broth to achieve a sauce-like consistency. Pour the purée into the pan with the whole lentils and mix well. Taste and adjust the seasoning. Cover to keep warm and set aside.

Season the salmon on both sides with salt and pepper. Place the fillets on a sheet pan and roast until just opaque throughout when tested with a knife tip, about 12 minutes; the timing will depending on the thickness of the fillets.

Mound the lentils on individual plates, dividing them evenly. Place a salmon fillet on top of each mound. Garnish with the parsley and basil and serve at once.

Coquilles Saint-Jacques à la Provençale

In Paris, a order of *coquilles Saint-Jacques* delivers sea scallops bathed in a creamy white wine sauce and elegantly served gratinéed in their shells. In this more casual recipe from Provence, the cream and cheese are replaced with tomatoes, olive oil, garlic, and basil, evoking thoughts of the warm coastal climate of southern France and its proximity to Italy.

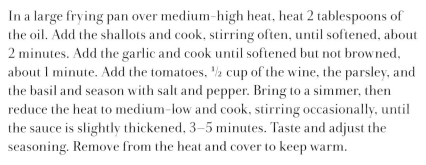

makes 4 servings

5 tablespoons olive oil

2 shallots, finely chopped

6 cloves garlic, minced

1 cup canned crushed tomatoes with juices

½ cup plus 2 tablespoons dry white wine

1 tablespoon finely chopped fresh flat-leaf parsley, plus more for garnish

1 tablespoon finely chopped fresh basil

Fine sea salt and freshly ground black pepper

¼ cup all-purpose flour

1½ lb sea scallops

In a large frying pan over medium-high heat, heat 2 tablespoons of the oil. Add the shallots and cook, stirring often, until softened, about 2 minutes. Add the garlic and cook until softened but not browned, about 1 minute. Add the tomatoes, ½ cup of the wine, the parsley, and the basil and season with salt and pepper. Bring to a simmer, then reduce the heat to medium-low and cook, stirring occasionally, until the sauce is slightly thickened, 3–5 minutes. Taste and adjust the seasoning. Remove from the heat and cover to keep warm.

Put the flour into a shallow bowl and season with salt and pepper. One at a time, dust the scallops with the seasoned flour, coating them evenly and tapping off the excess, and arrange in a single layer on a small sheet pan or large plate.

In a large, nonstick frying pan over medium-high heat, warm the remaining 3 tablespoons oil. Add the scallops and cook, tuning once, until golden brown on both sides and opaque throughout, about 2 minutes on each side. (If needed to prevent crowding, cook in two batches, then return all the scallops to the pan.) Add the remaining 2 tablespoons wine and deglaze the pan, scraping the pan bottom with a wooden spoon to dislodge any browned bits. Add the tomato sauce and stir gently to coat the scallops.

Transfer to a serving dish, garnish with parsley, and serve at once.

Braised Lamb Shanks with Potato-Celeriac Purée

One evening after a disastrous dinner party, Emily makes her way to Les Deux Compères and Gabriel. Over a glass of red wine, she shares with him that she's had it with trying to make people like her, so she might as well stop trying. "Well, there's just one problem," says Gabriel. "I like you." These braised lamb shanks and a good red wine are just the sort the thing you would find at a great Parisian restaurant. And with luck, you'll share them with someone as wonderful as Gabriel.

makes 4 servings

LAMB SHANKS

2 tablespoons olive oil

4 lamb shanks, each about 1 lb

Fine sea salt and freshly ground black pepper

1 carrot, peeled and finely chopped

1 yellow onion, finely chopped

2 celery ribs, finely chopped

3 small fresh thyme sprigs

1 bay leaf

3 cloves garlic, minced

2 tablespoons tomato paste

2 cups dry white wine

1 cup chicken broth

Finely grated zest and juice of 1 lemon

Finely grated zest and juice of 1 lime

Finely grated zest and juice of 1 orange

To make the lamb shanks, in a large Dutch oven or other heavy pot over medium-high heat, warm 1 tablespoon of the oil. While the oil heats, season the shanks all over with salt and pepper. Working in batches to avoid crowding, sear the shanks, turning as needed, until browned on all sides, 6–8 minutes. Transfer to a large plate. When all the shanks are browned, pour off the fat from the pot.

Preheat the oven to 250°F. Add the remaining 1 tablespoon oil to the pot and place over medium-low heat. Add the carrot, onion, and celery and cook, stirring occasionally, until softened, about 5 minutes. Add the thyme, bay leaf, garlic, tomato paste, ½ teaspoon salt, and a couple of grinds of pepper and stir for 1 minute. Add the wine, broth, and lemon and lime zests and juices and mix well.

Return the shanks to the pot and bring the liquid to a gentle simmer. Cover, transfer to the oven, and braise, turning the shanks every hour, until the meat is completely tender, about 2½ hours.

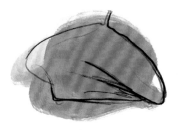

POTATO-CELERIAC PURÉE

1½ lb boiling potatoes, such as Yukon gold, peeled and cut into 1-inch chunks

1 celeriac (celery root), about ¾ lb, peeled and cut into 1-inch chunks

Fine sea salt

½ cup whole milk, warmed, plus more if needed

5 tablespoons unsalted butter, melted

About 30 minutes before the shanks are ready, begin making the purée. In a large saucepan, combine the potatoes, celery root, 1 tablespoon salt, and water to cover the vegetables by 1 inch. Bring to a boil over medium–high heat, then reduce the heat to medium and gently boil the vegetables, stirring every so often, until tender when pierced with a fork, 15–20 minutes. Drain well into a colander, then pass them through a ricer or food mill back into the hot pan. (Alternatively, return them to the hot pan and mash with a potato masher to a thick purée.) Using a fork or a whisk, beat the vegetables while gradually adding the milk and then the butter. Continue to beat vigorously with the fork or whisk until light and fluffy, adding more milk if needed to achieve a good consistency. Season with salt, then cover and keep warm.

Transfer the shanks to a heatproof platter and keep warm in the oven. Using a large metal spoon, skim the fat from the top of the cooking juices, then place the pot on the stove top over medium heat and simmer to reduce the cooking juice slightly. Stir in the orange zest and juice.

Divide the purée among 4 warmed individual plates. Top each with a lamb shank. Drizzle with the cooking juices and serve at once.

Seared Duck Breast with Cherry Sauce & Roasted Fingerlings

After booking a table at the Michelin-starred (and quite haughty) Le Grand Vefour for an important work dinner, Emily is horrified to learn that she mistakenly made the reservation for three months in the future. Fortunately, chef Gabriel comes to the rescue and agrees to seat them at Les Deux Compères. The epic meal, which includes this duck breast with cherry sauce and roasted fingerlings, is a smashing success. Serve with sautéed cremini mushrooms and a tangle of baby arugula.

makes 4 servings

DUCK BREASTS

4 skin-on duck breasts, each about ½ lb

Fine sea salt and freshly ground black pepper

1 tablespoon unsalted butter, at room temperature

1 tablespoon honey

POTATOES

1 lb small fingerling potatoes, halved lengthwise

3 tablespoons olive oil

1 tablespoon minced fresh rosemary leaves

Fine sea salt and freshly ground black pepper

3 cloves garlic, thinly sliced

CHERRY SAUCE

1 lb cherries, pitted (about 2 cups)

1 tablespoon grapeseed or canola oil

¼ cup chopped yellow onion

¼ cup finely chopped celery

1 tablespoon sherry vinegar

1 teaspoon peeled and grated fresh ginger

1 tablespoon honey

¼ teaspoon fine sea salt

To prepare each duck breast, using a sharp knife, make cuts through the skin and fat (but not into the meat) on the diagonal, spacing the cuts about ½ inch apart. Rotate the breast 90 degrees and cut the same way in the opposite direction to make a crosshatch pattern. Pat the duck breasts dry and sprinkle all over with salt and pepper. Let stand at room temperature for 30 minutes.

To make the potatoes, preheat the oven to 400°F. Pile the potatoes on a sheet pan. Drizzle with the oil, sprinkle with the rosemary, and season generously with salt and pepper, then turn the potatoes to coat evenly with the seasonings. Spread the potatoes in a single layer. Roast the potatoes for 10 minutes. Stir the potatoes and roast for 10 minutes more. Scatter the garlic over the potatoes and roast until the potatoes are golden brown and tender when pierced with a knife, about 10 minutes longer. Transfer to a platter and cover to keep warm.

While the potatoes roast, make the sauce. Measure ¼ cup of the cherries, cut them in half, and set aside. In a saucepan, heat the oil over medium-high heat. Add the onion and celery and cook, stirring often, until the onion is nearly translucent, about 3 minutes. Add the remaining cherries, the vinegar, and ginger, reduce the heat to medium, and cook, stirring and pressing against the cherries, until the cherries begin to break down and the mixture is slightly thickened, 4–5 minutes. Stir in the honey and salt and continue to cook, stirring, until the vegetables and cherries have softened and the mixture has thickened, 3–4 minutes. Remove from the heat, let cool slightly, then taste and adjust the seasoning.

continued on next page

continued from page 115

To cook the duck, smear the bottom of a large frying pan with the butter. Place the duck breasts, skin side down, in the cold pan and place over medium heat. Cook until the skin is crisp and golden, 7–8 minutes. Flip the breasts over and cook, brushing the crispy skin with the honey, until the second side is browned and the meat is cooked to medium-rare to medium (130°–135°F on an instant-read thermometer), 4–6 minutes. Using tongs, turn the breasts, one at a time, to sear each side until browned, about 1 minute on each side.

Transfer the duck breasts, skin side up, to a carving board (with a channel for capturing juices) and let rest for 5 minutes. Meanwhile, reheat the sauce over low heat, stirring, until warmed through. Stir in the reserved cherries.

Cut the duck breasts into ½-inch-thick slices. Arrange the duck on warmed individual plates or on a platter and drizzle with any duck juices. Spoon the warm roasted potatoes alongside the duck. Spoon some of the cherry sauce over the duck and serve at once. Pass the remaining sauce at the table.

Steak au Poivre with Potatoes Dauphinoise

Emily's first visit to the busy, adorable Les Deux Compères near her apartment is with Mindy, her new friend. They order a bottle of red wine and the quintessential French steak dish: *steak au poivre*. Emily decides her steak is too rare and tries to send it back. The waiter refuses her request, explaining that "the chef tells me that the steak is correct." But Emily presses on, only to discover that the chef is none other than her downstairs neighbor, Gabriel. He agrees to "happily burn it" for her but only after she tries it. She takes a bite and finds that she likes it. *Bon appétit*, ladies.

makes 4 servings

POTATOES DAUPHINOISE

1 clove garlic, crushed

3 tablespoons unsalted butter

2 lb russet potatoes

Fine sea salt and freshly ground black pepper

2 teaspoons minced fresh thyme

¼ lb Gruyère or Comté cheese, shredded

1 cup whole milk

STEAK AU POIVRE

⅓ cup freshly coarse-ground black pepper

4 New York strip steaks, each about ½ lb and 1½ inches thick

4 tablespoons unsalted butter

2 tablespoons olive oil

4 shallots, minced

3 tablespoons Cognac

½ cup red wine

1 cup beef or chicken broth

½ cup heavy cream

1 teaspoon Dijon mustard

Sea salt and freshly ground black pepper

Fresh flat-leaf parsley sprigs, for garnish

To make the potatoes, preheat the oven to 425°F. Rub the bottom and sides of a 2½-quart oval gratin dish or 9-inch square baking dish with the garlic, then coat the dish with 1 tablespoon of the butter.

Peel the potatoes, then cut crosswise into ⅛-inch-thick slices, preferably with a mandoline; do not rinse the potatoes. Arrange half of the potato slices, overlapping them slightly, in a single layer in the prepared pan. Sprinkle evenly with ½ teaspoon salt, ¼ teaspoon pepper, half of the thyme and then half of the cheese. Dot with 1 tablespoon of the butter, cut into small pieces. Top with the remaining potato slices in a single layer, overlapping them slightly, and top evenly with ½ teaspoon salt, ¼ teaspoon pepper, and the remaining 1 teaspoon thyme. Sprinkle evenly with the remaining cheese and then dot with the remaining 1 tablespoon butter, cut into small pieces.

In a small saucepan over medium-high heat, bring the milk just to a boil. Pour the milk evenly over the potato layers. Bake until the potatoes are easily pierced with a fork, the milk has been absorbed, and the top is slightly golden, 35–45 minutes. Transfer the dish to a wire rack and let stand for 5 minutes before serving.

While the potatoes are baking, begin preparing the steaks. Evenly sprinkle the steaks on both sides with the pepper, then press it into the meat, using your hands or the flat side of a cleaver blade. Cover and let stand at room temperature for 30 minutes.

continued on next page

continued from page 119

Select 1 large frying pan or 2 smaller frying pans big enough to accommodate the steaks without crowding. Place the pan or pans over medium-high heat, then melt the butter with the oil until bubbling, about 1 minute. Add the steaks and sear until browned on the underside, about 4 minutes. Flip the steaks over and sear on the second side until browned and an instant-read thermometer inserted into the thickest part registers 125°F for rare and 135°F for medium-rare, about 5 minutes longer. Transfer the steaks to a warmed platter and cover loosely with aluminum foil. If using 2 pans, combine any remaining fat into 1 pan.

Add the shallots to the pan and cook over medium-high heat, stirring often (and adding more butter if needed to prevent sticking), until softened, 2–3 minutes. Add the Cognac and cook until warmed, about 30 seconds. Remove the pan from the heat and use a long kitchen match to ignite the Cognac. When the alcohol has burned off, the flames will die out. (Keep a pan lid ready in case the flames flare up.) When the flames disappear, add the wine, bring to a boil, and cook, stirring occasionally, until lightly thickened, about 3 minutes. Add the broth, return the mixture to a boil, and cook until reduced by half and thickened to a sauce-like consistency, about 5 minutes longer. Whisk in the cream and mustard and simmer for 1 minute longer. Season with salt and pepper.

Transfer the steaks to warmed individual plates and spoon some of the sauce over each serving. Serve the potatoes dauphinoise alongside. Garnish the plates with parsley and serve.

"Quiche au Ciment" Deep-Dish Pizza

"I was in Chicago once," says Savoir founder Paul Brossard after meeting Emily for the first time in Sylvie's office, "and I ate the deep-dish pizza." "That is our specialty! We take a lot of pride," exclaims Emily. "It was *dégueulasse*. How do you say?" Paul responds. "Disgusting," helps Sylvie. "Like a quiche made of cement." But this cast-iron frying pan pizza is nothing like what Paul experienced. A thick, crisp cornmeal crust encases a wealth of savory toppings that perfectly represents the legendary Chicago pie.

---

makes 4 servings

DOUGH

3¾ cups bread flour, plus more for dusting

⅔ cup medium-grind cornmeal

1½ tablespoons sugar

1 tablespoon kosher salt

1 envelope (2¼ teaspoons) instant yeast

1½ cups lukewarm water (105°–115°F), plus more if needed

5 tablespoons olive oil, plus more for the bowl

TOPPINGS

¾ lb sweet or hot Italian sausages, casings removed

1 small red bell pepper, seeded and chopped

5 oz white or cremini mushrooms, brushed clean and sliced

Fine sea salt and freshly ground black pepper

Olive oil, for brushing

1½ oz pepperoni, sliced

⅓ cup oil-cured black olives, pitted and halved

1 cup tomato sauce

1¼ cups shredded low-moisture mozzarella cheese

To make the dough, in a bowl, stir together the flour, cornmeal, sugar, salt, and yeast. Add the water and oil and stir with a wooden spoon until the dough forms a ball; add a little water if it doesn't come together easily. Let rest for 5–10 minutes. Transfer the dough to a lightly floured work surface and knead for 5 minutes. The dough should be tacky to the touch but not sticky. Form it into a smooth ball. Oil a large bowl, put the dough into the bowl, turn the dough to coat it with oil, and then cover the bowl with plastic wrap. Let the dough rise in a warm place until doubled in bulk and spongy, about 2 hours.

Turn the dough out onto a lightly floured work surface, punch it down, and divide it in half. Shape each half into a smooth ball, dusting the dough with flour only if it becomes sticky. You will need only half of the dough for this recipe. Cover 1 ball with a clean kitchen towel and let it rest for 10 minutes. Place the second ball in a lock-top plastic freezer bag and freeze for up to 2 months. When ready to use, thaw at room temperature for 3–4 hours.

Position a rack in the lower third of the oven and preheat the oven to 400°F.

To prepare the toppings, line a plate with paper towels. In a frying pan over medium-high heat, fry the sausage, stirring occasionally and breaking up any clumps with a wooden spoon, until cooked through, about 8 minutes. Using a slotted spoon, transfer to the towel-lined plate to drain.

Pour off all but 1 tablespoon of the fat from the pan and return the pan to medium-high heat. Add the bell pepper and mushrooms, season with salt and pepper, and cook, stirring often, until softened and the

continued on next page

continued from page 123

mushrooms are browned around the edges, about 5 minutes. Remove from the heat and set aside.

Brush a 10-inch cast-iron frying pan with oil. Set the ball of dough in the center of the prepared pan and, using your hands, pat it into a thick disk. Then, continuing to use your hands, press the dough into the pan, easing it gently into an even layer on the bottom and about halfway up the sides. Brush the dough with more oil, then top evenly with the sausage, pepper and mushroom mixture, pepperoni, and olives. Pour the tomato sauce over the top, spread it evenly with the back of a spoon, and finish with the cheese. Season the whole pizza lightly with salt and pepper.

Transfer the pan to the oven and bake until the bottom of the dough is nicely browned (lift carefully with a spatula to peek), 20–25 minutes. Remove from the oven and let cool for 5 minutes. Slice directly in the pan and serve right away.

Provençal Beef Stew

Plenty of thyme, rosemary, and orange zest—the flavors of Provence—infuse this hearty beef stew cooked slowly in red wine. Dried porcini mushrooms and pancetta contribute an earthy richness to the dish. If you like, sauté a few handfuls of sliced fresh porcini, cremini, or trumpet mushrooms and stir them into the pot just before it comes off the stove. Ladle the stew over freshly cooked pasta, as here, or serve with mashed or roasted potatoes. And, of course, pour a good red wine to sip with the meal.

makes 6–8 servings

2 yellow onions

4 cloves garlic

4 lb boneless beef chuck roast, trimmed of excess fat and cut into 2-inch pieces

1 large carrot, quartered

1 long strip orange zest

8 fresh thyme sprigs

2 bay leaves

1 fresh rosemary sprig

Fine sea salt and freshly ground black pepper

1 bottle (750 ml) dry red wine

⅓ cup minced pancetta or bacon

2 tablespoons all-purpose flour

1 cup water

2 oz dried porcini mushrooms, roughly chopped

1 lb dried flat pasta, such as pappardelle

½ cup chopped fresh flat-leaf parsley

Quarter 1 onion and crush 2 garlic cloves. Add them to a large bowl along with the beef, carrot, orange zest, thyme, bay leaves, rosemary, and 1 teaspoon each salt and pepper. Pour in the wine and turn to mix and immerse the ingredients. Cover and refrigerate for at least 4 hours or up to overnight.

Finely chop the remaining onion and mince the remaining 2 garlic cloves. In a large Dutch oven or other heavy pot over medium-low heat, cook the pancetta, stirring occasionally, until the fat has rendered, about 5 minutes. Using a slotted spoon, transfer the pancetta to a small bowl. Raise the heat to medium, add the onion and garlic to the fat remaining in the pot, and cook, stirring occasionally, until the onion is translucent, 3–5 minutes. Using the slotted spoon, transfer to a large plate and set aside. Remove the pot from the heat.

Drain the beef mixture into a large, fine-mesh sieve set over a bowl. Remove the beef from the sieve and discard the other solids. Reserve the strained marinade. Pat the beef dry with paper towels; the wine will have tinted the beef purplish. Return the pot to medium-high heat. Working in batches, add the beef and cook, turning as needed, until browned on all sides, about 5 minutes. Using the slotted spoon, transfer the browned beef to the plate with the onion and garlic. When all the beef has been browned, add the flour to the pot and cook, stirring often, until browned, about 6 minutes.

continued on next page

continued from page 127

Raise the heat to high, gradually pour in the reserved marinade, bring to a boil, and deglaze the pot, scraping the pot bottom with a wooden spoon to dislodge any browned bits. Return the browned beef, onion and garlic mixture, and any accumulated juices to the pot. Add 1 teaspoon each salt and pepper and the water and bring almost to a boil. Reduce the heat to very low, cover, and simmer for 2 hours.

Add the mushrooms and continue to cook until the meat is tender enough to cut with a fork and the cooking liquid has thickened, 1–1½ hours longer. Using a large metal spoon, skim off some of the fat from the surface of cooking liquid, leaving some behind for flavor and richness.

Bring a large pot of salted water to a boil. Add the pasta, stir well, and cook, stirring occasionally, until al dente, according to the package directions. Drain well.

Divide the pasta evenly among warmed individual shallow bowls and ladle the stew over the top. Garnish with the parsley and serve.

Cheeseburger in Paris

Emily meets Judith Robertson from the American Friends of the Louvre (AFL) for lunch and is thrilled to see a menu in English with American offerings, snapping and then captioning her order #cheeseburgerinparadise. "The irony of how a French fry can make you feel so at home," exclaims Judith. The lunch also starts the wheels in motion for Pierre Cadault to donate a dress to the AFL auction at the Louvre, an event that brings Emily and Mathieu, Pierre's nephew, closer together and turns into a misfired PR stunt.

makes 6 burgers

GRILLED ONIONS

2 yellow onions, cut into ¼-inch-thick slices

1 tablespoon extra-virgin olive oil

Fine sea salt and freshly ground black pepper

½ teaspoon sugar

BURGERS

2 lb ground beef chuck

1 tablespoon Dijon mustard

1 tablespoon Worcestershire sauce

Fine sea salt and freshly ground black pepper

6 large slices cheddar or American cheese

6 hamburger buns, split

CONDIMENTS

Mayonnaise, ketchup, and/or mustard, for the buns

12 slices crisp fried bacon

About 3 handfuls torn butter or red leaf lettuce leaves

Tomato slices

To make the onions, prepare a gas or charcoal grill for direct and indirect grilling over medium-high heat (400°–450°F). Brush the grill grate clean.

Brush the onion slices on both sides with the oil. Arrange them on the grate directly over the fire and grill, turning once, until deeply grill marked, about 3 minutes on each side. Transfer the onion slices to a large piece of aluminum foil and season with ¼ teaspoon salt, ¼ teaspoon pepper, and the sugar. Fold the foil over the onions, crimping and sealing the foil to make a pouch, and then set the pouch on the grill grate away from the heat. Cook until tender, 15–20 minutes. Set aside while you make the burgers.

To make the burgers, in a bowl, combine the beef, mustard, Worcestershire sauce, ½ teaspoon salt and ½ teaspoon pepper and mix with your hands until well blended; do not overmix. Divide the mixture into 6 equal portions, then gently shape each portion into a patty no more than ¾ inch thick.

Place the patties on the grill grate directly over the fire, cover the grill, and grill, turning once after 4 minutes, for about 7 minutes total for medium. The burgers should be slightly pink at the center. Top each burger with a cheese slice 1 minute before the burgers are ready to come off the grill. To toast the buns, place them, cut side down, on the grate directly over the fire 1 minute before the burgers are ready. Transfer the burgers to a large plate and the buns, cut side up, to a work surface.

To serve, spread the cut side of the bun halves with the condiment(s) of choice. Place a burger on each bun bottom, then top with, in order, the grilled onions, bacon, and lettuce. Close with the bun tops and serve.

Strawberry Mousse

Fraises des bois, intensely flavored, tiny wild strawberries, hit Parisian markets in late spring and remain through summer. They are delicious on their own or served with a light sprinkle of sugar and whipped crème fraîche. When you aren't able to roam the markets of France, cultivated strawberries will have to do for this fluffy strawberry mousse, an excellent finale to an elegant dinner.

makes 6–8 servings

½ lb strawberries

⅓ cup sugar

¼ cup water

1 envelope (2½ teaspoons) unflavored gelatin

1 cup heavy cream

Set aside 4 strawberries for garnish. Stem and core the remaining strawberries, add them to a blender, and purée until smooth. Transfer the purée to a large bowl, passing it through a fine-mesh sieve if you don't want seeds in the mousse. Add the sugar and stir until the sugar dissolves.

In a small saucepan over high heat, bring the water to a boil. Remove from the heat, pour into a small bowl, and evenly sprinkle the gelatin over the top. Let stand until the gelatin softens, 3–5 minutes, then whisk until the gelatin dissolves. Whisk the gelatin mixture into the strawberry purée and let cool to room temperature.

In a bowl, using an electric mixer on medium speed or a hand whisk, whip the cream until soft peaks form. Using a rubber spatula, gently fold the whipped cream into the strawberry purée just until no white streaks remain. Spoon the mousse into 6–8 decorative dessert glasses or bowls, cover, and refrigerate for at least 2 hours or up to 2 days.

To serve, halve the reserved berries. Serve the mousse chilled, garnished with the strawberry slices.

Molten Chocolate Cakes

"You're sitting at the coolest café in all of Paris," says Thomas to Emily on the evening they meet at the Café de Flore. "At least, historically." Thomas, a sexy semiotics professor, goes on to tell Emily about Jean-Paul Sartre and Simone de Beauvoir, who frequented the café after Les Deux Magots—the hangout of Hemingway and Picasso—became "too bourgeois." As they sip wine and Thomas enjoys a slice of decadent chocolate cake, their conversation and the evening heats up. These simple yet elegant cakes can do the same for your evening.

makes 6 servings

4 tablespoons unsalted butter, cut into small pieces, plus more for the ramekins

2 tablespoons unsweetened natural cocoa powder, sifted, plus more for the ramekins

8 oz bittersweet chocolate, finely chopped

1 teaspoon pure vanilla extract

Pinch of fine sea salt

4 large egg yolks

6 tablespoons granulated sugar

3 large egg whites

Confectioners' sugar, for dusting

Preheat the oven to 400°F. Lightly butter six ¾-cup ramekins and then dust with cocoa powder, tapping out the excess. Set the ramekins on a small sheet pan.

Combine the chocolate and butter in a heatproof bowl and set over (not touching) barely simmering water in a saucepan. Heat, stirring often, just until the chocolate and butter melt and the mixture is glossy and smooth. Remove from over the water and stir in the vanilla and salt. Set aside to cool slightly.

In a large bowl, using an electric mixer on medium-high speed, beat together the egg yolks, 3 tablespoons of the granulated sugar, and the 2 tablespoons cocoa powder until thick and smooth. Add the chocolate mixture to the yolk mixture and continue to beat on medium speed until blended. The mixture will be very thick.

In a bowl, using clean beaters, beat the egg whites on medium-high speed until very foamy and thick. Sprinkle in the remaining 3 tablespoons granulated sugar, increase the speed to high, and beat until firm, glossy peaks form. Spoon half of the beaten whites onto the chocolate mixture and stir in just until blended. Using a rubber spatula, gently fold in the remaining whites just until no white streaks remain. Spoon into the prepared ramekins.

Bake the cakes until they are puffed and the tops are cracked, about 13 minutes. The inside of the cracks will look slightly wet.

Remove from the oven and dust with confectioners' sugar. Alternatively, run a small knife around the inside edge of each ramekin to loosen the cake sides, then invert a dessert plate over the ramekin, invert the ramekin and plate together, lift off the ramekin, and dust with the confectioners' sugar. Serve at once.

QUATRE
LA PÂTISSERIE

Palmiers

When Emily pitches Chicago hotelier Randy Zimmer on the idea of a custom fragrance created by Maison Lavaux, she likens having a signature scent in his hotels to selling a house: "The one thing you should do is bake cookies. The smell reminds people of home and warmth . . . and sugar, and butter, and a happy place. You need some cookies, Randy." Baking a batch of these buttery, sugar-dusted, crisp cookies—a staple at many French bakeries—could sell any house—and maybe perfume too.

makes about 10 palmiers

2 tablespoons unsalted butter, melted and cooled

½ teaspoon pure vanilla extract

½ cup granulated sugar

½ cup confectioners' sugar

1 sheet frozen puff pastry, about ½ lb, thawed according to package directions

Preheat the oven to 375°F. Line 1 sheet pan with parchment paper.

In a small bowl, stir together the butter and vanilla. In a medium bowl, using a fork, stir together the granulated and confectioners' sugars. Measure out ½ cup of the sugar mixture and set aside.

Sprinkle 3 tablespoons of the remaining sugar mixture onto a work surface. Place the puff pastry on top of the sugared surface. Sprinkle more of the sugar mixture on top of the pastry, spreading it evenly with your hands. Using a rolling pin and starting at the center of the pastry sheet, roll out the pastry into a 10×20-inch rectangle, always rolling from the center outward and rotating the sheet a quarter turn after every one or two passes with the pin. As you work, sprinkle a little more sugar mixture underneath and on top of the pastry as needed to prevent sticking.

Using a pastry brush, brush the butter mixture over the surface of the pastry. Sprinkle evenly with the reserved ½ cup sugar mixture. Starting at one short end, fold a band of the pastry 2 inches wide over onto itself. Repeat this folding until you reach the center of the pastry. Fold the other end of the rectangle toward the center in the same way. Fold 1 folded half on top of the other folded half (as if closing a book) and cut crosswise into slices ½ inch thick. Place the slices, cut side down, on the prepared pan, spacing them about 2 inches apart.

Bake the palmiers until golden, about 15 minutes. Let cool on the pan on a wire rack for 5 minutes, then transfer them to the rack and let cool completely.

Butter Croissants

Grabbing breakfast with Mindy in one of the many little Parisian cafés that they frequent, Emily orders a coffee, some fruit, *"et un croissant avec le préservatif,"* only to find out that *préservatif* doesn't mean yummy fruit preserves but condoms. The waiter derisively explains the meaning to her in English and then stalks away. Fortunately for Emily, she still gets her buttery croissant. These are an adventure to make, but there's also nothing like the pride you'll feel when serving your own freshly baked croissants.

makes 16 croissants

Croissant Dough (page 212)

Unsalted butter, for the sheet pans

1 large egg

1 tablespoon whole milk

Make the croissant dough as directed. Lightly butter 2 half sheet pans (18×13 inches).

To form the croissants, roll out the dough on a lightly floured work surface into a 9×18-inch rectangle. Cut the rectangle in half lengthwise and then cut each half crosswise into 4-inch squares for a total of 8 squares. Cut each square in half on the diagonal.

Working with 1 dough triangle at a time, gently stretch the triangle to about twice its original length. Then gently stretch the wide end of the triangle. Lay the triangle on your work surface with the point facing you. Place your hands at the top on the wide end and gently roll the dough toward you. Just before you get to the point, smear the tip with your thumb and then continue to roll until the tip is under the croissant. Place tip down on a prepared sheet pan. For the classic shape, turn the ends of the croissant in slightly toward the center. Repeat with the remaining triangles, spacing them 2–3 inches apart on the sheet pans. (At this point, the shaped pastries can be covered and frozen on the sheet pans and then transferred to lock-top plastic freezer bags and frozen for up to 1 month; thaw in the refrigerator overnight, then let rise and bake as directed.)

Cover the sheet pan loosely with a kitchen towel and let the pastries rise at room temperature until they double in bulk, about 1½ hours.

Preheat the oven to 425°F. In a small bowl, lightly beat the egg with the milk to make an egg wash. Lightly brush the tops of the pastries with the egg wash. Bake the pastries, 1 sheet pan at a time, until golden brown, 15–18 minutes. Let the pastries cool on the pans on wire racks.

Serve warm or at room temperature. The baked croissants will keep in an airtight container at room temperature for up to 1 day; reheat in a 300°F oven for about 5 minutes before serving.

Apple Frangipane Tart

Thanks to purchased puff pastry, this elegant tart couldn't be easier to throw together. The marriage of crisp and airy pastry, nutty-sweet almond frangipane, and thinly sliced apples is a guaranteed showstopper. To up your game, add a dollop of lightly whipped crème fraîche to each serving.

makes 8 servings

1½ cups sliced almonds

All-purpose flour, for dusting

1 sheet frozen puff pastry, about 1 lb, thawed according to package instructions

⅔ cup sugar

¼ teaspoon kosher salt

2 large eggs, lightly beaten

1 teaspoon pure vanilla extract

1 teaspoon pure almond extract

2 tablespoons unsalted butter, melted and cooled

2 large baking apples, such as Pink Lady or Gala

Juice of ½ lemon

¼ cup apricot jam, for glazing

Position a rack in the upper third of the oven and preheat the oven to 425°F. Line a large sheet pan (ideally 16×12 inches) with parchment paper. Spread the almonds into an even layer on the prepared sheet pan and bake, stirring once or twice, until lightly toasted, about 5 minutes. Transfer to a bowl. Let the sheet pan cool completely.

On a lightly floured work surface, roll out the puff pastry into a rectangle just large enough to fit on the sheet pan. Trim the edges even with a sharp knife or pastry cutter. Transfer to the prepared pan, fold over the edges (about ¼ inch) to form a rim, and pinch together. Refrigerate while you make the frangipane.

In a food processor, combine the almonds, sugar, and salt and process until the almonds are finely ground. Add the eggs, vanilla and almond extracts, and butter and process until the mixture comes together. Set aside.

Prick the chilled puff pastry all over with a fork. Bake until it looks dried out and very lightly browned, about 8 minutes. Remove from the oven and reduce the oven temperature to 350°F.

While the pastry bakes, peel and core the apples, then cut crosswise into very thin slices. Transfer to a bowl and toss with the lemon juice, coating evenly.

Smear the frangipane in a thin, even layer on the pastry and arrange the apple slices, overlapping them slightly, decoratively on top. Bake until the tart is golden and the apples are tender-crisp, about 30 minutes. Transfer the pan to a wire rack.

To glaze the tart, heat the jam in a saucepan over low heat until it liquefies. Pour through a fine-mesh sieve set over a small bowl. Gently brush the top of the warm tart with a thin coating of the jam.

Cut into rectangles and serve warm or at room temperature.

Un Pain au Chocolat

On her second day in Paris, Emily heads to Boulangerie Moderne for breakfast, where she is taken with all the tantalizing pastries. The woman working behind the counter does her best to help Emily pronounce *un pain au chocolat*, but Emily is only focused on devouring the rich, buttery treat. Made from croissant dough, this iconic pastry conceals a gooey stripe of bittersweet chocolate within its flaky layers.

makes 12 pastries

Croissant Dough (page 212)

Unsalted butter, for the sheet pans

All-purpose flour, for dusting

6 oz bittersweet or semisweet chocolate, chopped

1 large egg

1 tablespoon whole milk

Make the croissant dough as directed. Lightly butter 2 half sheet pans (18×13 inches).

On a lightly floured work surface, roll out the dough into a 12×16-inch rectangle. Cut the dough lengthwise into 3 equal strips, then cut each strip crosswise into 4 squares, for a total of 12 squares. Working with 1 square at a time, place a rounded tablespoon of the chocolate in a strip down the middle of the square. Fold the bottom third up and then fold the top down so it slightly overlaps the bottom flap. Pinch the seam to seal. Place, seam side down, on a prepared sheet pan. Repeat with the remaining dough squares and chocolate, spacing the pastries 2–3 inches apart. (At this point, the shaped pastries can be covered and frozen on the sheet pans and then transferred to lock-top plastic freezer bags and frozen for up to 1 month; let thaw in the refrigerator overnight, then let rise and bake as directed.)

Cover loosely with a kitchen towel and let the pastries rise at room temperature until they double in bulk, about 1½ hours.

Preheat the oven to 425°F. In a small bowl, lightly beat the egg with the milk to make an egg wash. Lightly brush the tops of the pastries with the egg wash. Bake the pastries, 1 sheet pan at a time, until golden brown, 15–18 minutes. Let the pastries cool on the pans on wire racks.

Serve warm or at room temperature. The baked pastries will keep in an airtight container at room temperature for up to 1 day; reheat in a 300°F oven for about 5 minutes before serving.

Honey Madeleines

Cake-like madeleines, with their distinctive shell shape, are sold in many Parisian boulangeries and patisseries. They are also wonderfully easy to make at home when popping out to the local boulangerie isn't an option! This version is delicately flavored with honey and orange flower water, but you can swap out the orange flower water for 1 teaspoon pure vanilla extract if you like. Look for a madeleine pan in a well-stocked cookware shop or online.

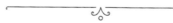

makes 12 madeleines

5 tablespoons unsalted butter, melted and cooled

½ cup cake flour, plus more for the pan

1 large egg

3 tablespoons sugar

2 tablespoons honey

2 teaspoons orange flower water

½ teaspoon baking powder

Position a rack in the lower third of the oven and preheat the oven to 400°F. Using a pastry brush and 1 tablespoon of the butter, coat the 12 molds of a madeleine pan with a thick, even layer of butter, making sure you reach into each and every ridge. Dust the molds with flour, tilting the pan to coat all the surfaces and then turning it upside down over the kitchen sink and tap it gently to knock out the excess flour.

In a bowl, using an electric mixer on medium speed, beat together the egg and sugar for 30 seconds. Increase the speed to high and beat until very thick and quadrupled in volume, about 10 minutes. Add the honey and orange flower water and beat until combined. Turn off the mixer. Sift together the flour and baking powder over the egg mixture, then, using a rubber spatula, fold in the flour mixture. Gently fold in the remaining 4 tablespoons butter, mixing evenly.

Scoop a heaping tablespoon of the batter into each mold. Each mold should be three-fourths full. Bake the cakes until golden brown at the edges and the tops spring back when lightly touched, 10–12 minutes. Invert the pan onto a wire rack and tap to release the madeleines. If any of them stick, use a butter knife to loosen the edges, then invert and tap again.

Serve slightly warm. Madeleines are best eaten the same day they are baked. If you need to store them, they will keep in an airtight container at room temperature for up to 3 days.

Peanut Butter Sablés

When Emily finally receives her "American _paquets_" in the mail, she is thrilled. After lugging them up five flights of stairs—with the help of hunky Gabriel—she opens the first one only to discover her Trader Joe's organic chunky peanut butter has exploded inside the box. Never fear, Emily! Just make these delicious peanut butter cookies that recall the crunchy, crumbly, buttery _sablés_ of Normandy. Of course, the French would never dream of adding peanut butter to cookie dough.

makes about 40 cookies

½ cup unsalted butter, preferably European-style, at room temperature

½ cup granulated sugar

¼ cup firmly packed light brown sugar

½ teaspoon fine sea salt

1 cup unsweetened, unsalted chunky peanut butter

1 large egg

1 teaspoon pure vanilla extract

1 cup all-purpose flour

Flaky salt and turbinado sugar, for finishing (optional)

In a large bowl, using an electric mixer on medium speed, beat together the butter, granulated and brown sugars, and salt until smooth and fluffy, about 3 minutes. Add the peanut butter, egg, and vanilla and beat until well blended. On low speed, add the flour and mix just until fully incorporated.

Divide the dough in half. Form half into a rough log, wrap the log in a piece of plastic wrap, and, using your hands, roll it into a smooth log about 2 inches in diameter and 6 inches long. Twist the ends to seal. Repeat with the second half of dough to form a second log. Refrigerate the logs until firm, at least 3 hours or up to overnight.

Preheat the oven to 350°F. Line 2 sheet pans with parchment paper.

Unwrap the dough logs and reroll each log on a flat work surface to smooth the surface and to make it as evenly round as possible. If you like, spread a little turbinado sugar on a plate and roll each log in the sugar, coating evenly. Trim off both ends of each log so they are flat and smooth, then cut the logs crosswise into ¼-inch-thick slices. Arrange the cookies on the prepared sheet pans, spacing them at least 1 inch apart. Sprinkle the cookies with a little flaky salt and turbinado sugar, if using, pressing them lightly into the dough.

Bake the cookies, 1 sheet pan at a time, until the bottoms are golden brown, 12–15 minutes. Let the cookies cool briefly on the pans on wire racks, then transfer to the racks to cool completely. The cookies will keep in an airtight container at room temperature for up to 1 week.

Baguettes

The Boulangerie Moderne plays a deliciously recurring role throughout the series, with inviting glass cases of French pastries and rows of fresh baguettes lining the walls. Made from only a handful of ingredients, baguette dough needs time to develop flavor. Start by making a sponge and letting it sit overnight to ferment. Your patience will be rewarded. A wedge of cheese, some good wine, and a homemade baguette and your picnic is ready—even better if that picnic is in Jardin du Palais Royal.

make 3 baguettes

SPONGE

1 package (2¼ teaspoons) active dry yeast

1½ cups lukewarm water (105°–115°F)

1 teaspoon malt syrup or sugar

2 cups bread flour

DOUGH

2 cups bread flour, plus more for dusting

1½ teaspoons sea salt

¼ cup cornmeal or semolina flour

To make the sponge, in the bowl of a stand mixer, dissolve the yeast in the lukewarm water, then add the malt syrup. Using a wooden spoon, stir in the flour until the mixture is smooth. Cover the bowl with plastic wrap and let stand for at least 3 hours at cool room temperature or for up to overnight in the refrigerator. If refrigerated, remove from the refrigerator and let warm to room temperature for 1 hour before finishing the dough.

To make the dough, add the flour and salt to the sponge and stir with the dough hook until the mixture comes together in a shaggy mass. Place the bowl on the mixer stand, attach the dough hook, and knead the dough on low speed until smooth and elastic, 5–10 minutes. Periodically stop the mixer and scrape down the bowl sides and the dough hook before continuing. Remove the bowl from the mixer stand and scrape the dough down evenly. Cover the bowl with plastic wrap and let the dough rise in a warm, draft-free spot until it doubles in bulk, 1½–2 hours. The dough will look puffy and feel soft when you gently poke it with a finger.

Punch down the dough. Re-cover the bowl and let the dough rise again until doubled in bulk, 30–45 minutes. Then turn the dough out onto a clean work surface and divide it into thirds. Shape each third into a loose, round ball. Cover the balls with a kitchen towel and let rest for 5 minutes before shaping.

Lightly dust a large sheet pan with the cornmeal. Working with 1 ball of dough at a time, pick up the ball and slap it hard onto a clean work surface. If the dough feels dry, spritz it with a little water from a mister. Evenly flatten the dough ball with the heel of your hand. Roll the top third down onto itself and seal it by pushing it gently with the heel of your hand. Continue rolling and sealing the dough until you have an oval loaf. Then, using both hands, and starting in the center and working outward, elongate the loaf by rolling it gently against the work surface with even pressure until it is as long as the prepared sheet pan. Transfer the loaf to the sheet pan. Repeat with the remaining balls of dough and add the loaves to the pan, spacing them evenly apart.

Cover the loaves loosely with a damp kitchen towel and leave to rise in a warm, draft-free spot until doubled in size, 30–40 minutes. The loaves should feel light and spongy when gently squeezed.

Position a rack in the lower third of the oven and preheat the oven to 500°F.

Using a single-edged razor blade or a sharp serrated knife, make 4 or 5 slashes down the length of each baguette, holding the blade at a shallow (45-degree) angle so you slit just under the surface of the dough. Quickly mist the loaves generously with water.

Immediately slide the pan into the oven and reduce the heat to 450°F. Bake the loaves until they are golden brown and sound hollow when tapped on the bottom, 20–25 minutes. If they are not baking evenly, rotate the pan back to front halfway through baking. Let the loaves cool on the pan on a wire rack for at least 20 minutes before serving.

Although they are best eaten fresh, baguettes can be well wrapped and frozen for up to 2 weeks, then thawed at room temperature for 15 minutes and refreshed in a 400°F oven for 10–15 minutes.

Pan Bagnat

With the Pierre Cadault and Grey Space debacle still fresh in everyone's mind, Mathieu surprises Emily with a boat tour (on his own boat!) of Paris along the Seine (romantic anyone?). A bottle of Champagne, a baguette, and some cheese appear, and Emily starts to ponder what might happen between them. This signature sandwich of Nice—stuffed with tuna, tomatoes, hard-boiled eggs, olives, and plenty of crunchy vegetables—is as Gallic as it gets and is the ideal meal for tucking into a picnic basket stowed at the back of a boat.

makes 4 servings

4 large, round, chewy coarse country rolls

½ cup extra-virgin olive oil

2 tablespoons red wine vinegar

4–8 delicate lettuce leaves, such as butter, red leaf, or green leaf

1 can (5 oz) olive oil–packed tuna, drained and flaked

1 small raw or roasted red bell pepper, seeded and cut into narrow slices

2 hard-boiled eggs, peeled and thinly sliced crosswise

2 large, ripe tomatoes, thinly sliced

½ small cucumber, peeled and thinly sliced

½ small red onion, sliced paper-thin

¼ cup sliced pitted olives, preferably a mix of black and green

Using a serrated knife, halve the rolls horizontally. Arrange cut side up on a work surface, then drizzle the cut sides with the oil and vinegar.

Place 1 or 2 lettuce leaves on each of the roll bottoms. Arrange the tuna, bell pepper, eggs, tomatoes, cucumber, onion, and olives on top of the lettuce, dividing them evenly. Close with the roll tops, cut side down, and serve at once. For a more traditional pan bagnant, wrap each sandwich in parchment paper or aluminum foil, then wrap with plastic wrap or place in a plastic bag. Weight the sandwich with a cast-iron pan or other heavy pot for 20 minutes, turning the sandwich halfway through. Serve at once or refrigerate and serve within 8 hours.

Savory Ham & Mushroom Crêpes

Strolling through the streets of Paris at night while enjoying a crêpe from a street stand is magical, especially if you are on the arm of Mathieu Cadault, one of the city's most sought-after bachelors. "It's funny how every culture has its pancake," observes Emily. Mathieu scoffs, "You can't compare our crêpes to your pancakes. I mean, no contest. We win." These buckwheat crêpes—filled with *jambon de Paris*, sautéed mushrooms, and Gruyère—are indeed incomparable.

makes 10 crêpes

BUCKWHEAT CRÊPES

3 large eggs

1¾ cups whole milk

½ cup buckwheat flour

¾ cup all-purpose flour

4 tablespoons unsalted butter, melted and cooled, plus more for cooking and for the sheet pan

½ teaspoon fine sea salt

FILLING

1 tablespoon unsalted butter

1 large shallot, finely chopped

Fine sea salt and freshly ground black pepper

½ lb cremini or button mushrooms, brushed clean and sliced

5 thin slices ham (about 5 oz), preferably jambon de Paris, cut in half

⅓ lb Gruyère cheese, shredded

Snipped fresh chives, for garnish

To make the crêpe batter, in a blender or food processor, combine all the ingredients and process until well blended. Scrape down the sides of the blender or processor bowl and process again until very smooth. Cover and refrigerate for at least 4 hours or up to overnight. Let the batter come to room temperature for 30 minutes before cooking.

Heat an 8- or 9-inch nonstick frying pan or crêpe pan over medium heat until hot. Brush the pan lightly with butter. Pour ¼ cup batter into the middle of the hot pan and immediately swirl the batter into a thin, even layer (a small spatula will help spread it). Cook until the edges are crisp and the underside is golden. Then, using a spatula, turn the crêpe and cook until golden on the second side, for a total of 1–3 minutes, depending on how hot your pan is. Transfer to a plate. Repeat with the remaining batter. You will need only 10 crêpes for this recipe. To store the remainder, let them cool, then stack them, separating them with pieces of waxed paper, wrap the stack in plastic wrap, and refrigerate for up to 3 days. Before using, bring to room temperature, then heat the same frying pan over medium heat, brush with butter, and heat each crêpe, turning once, just until warm before filling.

Preheat the oven to 375°F. Brush a large sheet pan generously with butter.

To make the filling, in a frying pan over medium heat, melt the butter. Add the shallot, season with salt, and cook, stirring often, until tender, about 2 minutes. Add the mushrooms and cook, stirring often, until tender, about 5 minutes. Remove from the heat.

To assemble the crêpes, place ½ slice of ham on one-fourth of each crêpe. Add 1 heaping tablespoon grated cheese, spreading it on top of the ham. Then top the cheese with 1 heaping tablespoon of the mushrooms. Fold the crêpe in half and then in half again over the filling to form a triangle. Arrange the filled crêpes on the prepared sheet pan. Warm the crêpes in the oven until the cheese is melted and the crêpes are crisp, 10–13 minutes. Serve at once, garnished with the chives.

#OhCrêpe

"Oh when you dropped your crêpe!" sighs Mindy, looking at her phone. "Hashtag oh crêpe!" exclaim Emily and Mindy in unison as they reminisce over Emily's (briefly) soon-to-be-deleted Instagram account @emilyinparis. A *crêpe sucrée*—"sweet crepe"—is always a treat. Serve these classic thin French pancakes filled with butter, sugar, and fresh lemon juice, or make them naughtier with a smear of Nutella and some sliced bananas or strawberries.

makes about 16 crêpes

CRÊPES

1 cup whole milk

³/₄ cup all-purpose flour

2 large eggs

2 tablespoons unsalted butter, melted and cooled, plus more for cooking

¹/₄ teaspoon fine sea salt

FILLINGS

Room-temperature unsalted butter, superfine sugar, and fresh lemon juice

Nutella and sliced bananas or strawberries

To make the crêpe batter, combine all of the ingredients in a blender and blend on high speed until smooth. There should be no flour lumps. Refrigerate for 30 minutes, then blend again at high speed for 1 minute.

Heat an 8- or 9-inch nonstick frying pan or crêpe pan over medium heat until hot. Brush the pan lightly with butter. Pour ¹/₄ cup of the batter into the middle of the hot pan and immediately swirl the batter into a thin, even layer (a small spatula will help spread it). Cook until the edges are crisp and the underside is golden. Then, using a spatula, turn the crêpe and cook until golden on the second side, for a total of 1–3 minutes, depending on how hot your pan is. Transfer to a plate. Repeat with the remaining batter.

Serve the crêpes warm with the filling of your choice: Spread each crêpe lightly with butter, then sprinkle lightly with sugar and lemon juice and fold into quarters. Or spread with Nutella, arrange banana or strawberry slices on half of the crêpe, and fold into quarters.

To store unfilled crêpes, let them cool, then stack them, separating them with pieces of waxed paper, wrap the stack in plastic wrap, and refrigerate for up to 3 days. Or wrap the stacked crêpes in aluminum foil, place in a lock-top plastic freezer bag, and freeze for up to 2 months, then thaw in the refrigerator. To reheat, heat the same frying pan over medium heat, brush with butter, and heat each crêpe, turning once, just until warm.

Vanilla Macarons

French *macarons* deliver the perfect balance of crisp and chewy, and because they are made with almond flour, they are also gluten-free. This vanilla-scented version is sandwiched with white chocolate buttercream. You can swap out the vanilla extract for another flavor, such as peppermint or lemon. Many Parisian patisseries display *macarons* in a rainbow of colors. Add a few drops of gel food coloring in your favorite color to create your own brilliant hue. Make the *macarons* a day in advance of serving, as they need at least a full day in the refrigerator to soften to their classic chewy texture.

makes 24 sandwich cookies

2 cups confectioners' sugar

1⅓ cups superfine almond flour

3 large egg whites

1 teaspoon pure vanilla extract

½ teaspoon pure almond extract

¼ teaspoon cream of tartar

⅛ teaspoon salt

White Chocolate Buttercream (page 214)

Line 2 sheet pans with parchment paper. Using a 1½-inch round template such as a biscuit cutter, draw 24 circles on each parchment sheet, spacing them about 1 inch apart. Turn the parchment paper over. Combine 1 cup of the sugar and the almond flour in a sifter or fine-mesh sieve. Set aside.

In a large bowl, using an electric mixer on medium speed, beat together the egg whites, vanilla and almond extracts, cream of tartar, and salt on medium speed until soft peaks, about 3 minutes. On high speed, gradually beat in the remaining 1 cup sugar, beating until stiff peaks form, about 2 minutes longer.

Sift about one-third of the sugar–almond flour mixture over the beaten whites. Using a rubber spatula, gently fold it in just until blended. Repeat to fold in the remaining confectioners' sugar mixture in two more additions until incorporated. Continue to fold the mixture just until all the ingredients are fully blended and the batter flows in a slow, thick ribbon when the spatula is lifted.

Transfer the batter to a piping bag fitted with a ⅜-inch round tip. Holding the piping bag with the tip about ½ inch above a prepared sheet pan, pipe mounds of the batter onto each pan, using the circles as a guide. Make the mounds as smooth as possible by moving the bag off to one side after piping each mound. Gently smooth any pointy tips with a damp fingertip. Tap each sheet pan firmly against the work surface two or three times to release any air bubbles. Let the cookies stand at room temperature until they look less wet and are a little tacky, 45–60 minutes.

continued on page 165

continued from page 162

Preheat the oven to 300°F.

Place 1 sheet pan in the oven and bake the cookies until they rise and set but are not browned, about 20 minutes. The bottoms of the cookies should be dry and firm to the touch and not stick to the parchment paper. If they stick, bake them for a few minutes longer. Let cool on the pan on a wire rack for 1 minute, then use a metal spatula to move the cookies directly to the rack. Repeat to bake the second pan of cookies the same way. Let cool completely.

Make the buttercream as directed.

Turn half of the cookies bottom side up on a work surface. Spread about 1 teaspoon of the buttercream over each bottom. Top them with the remaining cookies, bottom side down, pressing lightly. (You will have leftover buttercream; use it to transform purchased cookies into sandwich cookies or to dress up pound cake. Place the macarons in a single layer on a sheet pan, cover with plastic wrap, and refrigerate for at least 1 day or up to 3 days before serving. (Or place in the freezer until frozen, then stack them in an airtight container and freeze for up to 6 months; thaw in the refrigerator before serving.) Serve chilled or at cool room temperature.

Raspberry Custard Tartlets

While purchasing a bouquet of pretty pink roses, Emily meets Camille, a friendly French woman (who later turns out to be Gabriel's girlfriend!). They pop in to Camille's favorite boulangerie-patisserie for coffee. Lining the shelves are all kinds of tempting treats, including luscious strawberry and raspberry custard tarts that are as pretty as a bouquet of flowers. Each of these tartlets is a perfect single serving, or you can make a 10-inch tart with the same ingredients. If you like, substitute strawberries for the raspberries.

makes 6 tartlets

Tarte Dough (page 213)

Pastry Cream (page 213)

2 pints raspberries

Confectioners' sugar, for dusting

Make the dough and chill as directed. Have ready six 4-inch round tartlet pans with removable bottoms. Divide the dough into 6 equal pieces (each about 2 oz), then flatten each piece into a thick disk. On a lightly floured work surface, roll out each dough disk into a round about 6 inches in diameter and 1/8 inch thick. Transfer the rounds to the tartlet pans, easing each one into a pan and patting it firmly into the bottom and up the sides. Roll the rolling pin over the top of each pan, neatly trimming off the excess dough. Place the tartlet shells on a sheet pan and refrigerate or freeze until firm, about 30 minutes.

Preheat the oven to 375°F. Line the tartlet shells with aluminum foil or parchment paper and fill with pie weights or dried beans. Bake until the shells start to look dry and lightly golden, about 15 minutes. Remove the weights and foil and continue baking until golden brown, 5–7 minutes longer. Let cool completely on a wire rack.

Make the pastry cream and chill as directed.

Carefully remove the cooled tartlet shells from the pans. Stir the chilled pastry cream until smooth. Spoon into the bottom of the tartlet shells and spread evenly. (You may have a little extra pastry cream, depending on the depth of your tartlet pans. It will keep for up to 3–4 days and can be eaten like pudding.) Arrange the raspberries in concentric circles on the pastry cream. Dust with confectioners' sugar and serve.

Tarte au Citron

Nearly every bakery in Paris will have this iconic tart of delicate, buttery pastry and creamy, lip-puckering lemon curd on offer. The lemon curd is fully cooked on the stove top and can be used in other ways as well, such as filling for cake layers or sandwich cookies, spread on freshly baked scones, rolled into crêpes, or just decadently eaten from a spoon.

makes 6–8 servings

Tarte Dough (page 213)

LEMON CURD

3 large whole eggs plus 3 large egg yolks, lightly beaten

¾ cup sugar

¾ cup fresh lemon juice, strained (about 6 large lemons)

2 tablespoons finely grated lemon zest

¾ cup unsalted butter, cut into pieces

WHIPPED CREAM

1 cup heavy cream

2 tablespoons sugar

½ teaspoon pure vanilla extract

Make the dough and chill as directed. On a lightly floured work surface, roll out the dough into a round about 12 inches in diameter and ⅛ inch thick. Roll the dough around the rolling pin, then unroll the dough over a 9½-inch tart pan with a removable bottom and ease the dough into the pan, patting it firmly into the bottom and up the sides. Roll the pin over the top of the pan, neatly trimming off the excess dough. Refrigerate or freeze the tart shell until firm, about 30 minutes.

Preheat the oven to 375°F. Line the tart shell with aluminum foil or parchment paper and fill with pie weights or dried beans. Bake until the shell starts to look dry, about 15 minutes. Remove the weights and foil and continue baking until golden brown, about 15 minutes longer. Let cool completely on a wire rack.

To make the lemon curd, in a heavy, nonreactive saucepan over low heat, combine all the ingredients and cook slowly, stirring constantly with a heatproof rubber spatula, until the butter melts and the mixture is thick enough to coat the spatula, 7–8 minutes.

Remove from the heat and strain through a fine-mesh sieve into the cooled tart shell. Spread the curd into an even layer. Cover the tart with plastic wrap, pressing it directly onto the surface of the filling. Refrigerate the tart until chilled, at least 2 hours or up to overnight.

To make the whipped cream, in a bowl, using an electric mixer on medium speed, beat together the cream, sugar, and vanilla until medium peaks form. Use right away, or cover with plastic wrap and refrigerate for up to 4 hours, then whisk the cream briefly before using.

To serve the tart, remove the pan sides and slide the tart off the pan bottom onto a serving plate. Let stand at room temperature for about 20 minutes. Mound the whipped cream on top of the tart, cut into wedges, and serve.

CINQ
LE CAFÉ

Chicago Cocktail
with Beer Nuts

In one of the first scenes of season 1, Emily arrives at a Chicago Cubs bar to meet up with then-boyfriend Doug just in time to see the Cubs make it to the playoffs. Between shouts of joy, beers, and bar-top bowls of nuts, Emily orders a glass of wine, "White wine. Anything French if you have it." She then proceeds to tell Doug that she's got some "crazy news": her boss, Madeleine, is pregnant, so she's taking Madeleine's job in Paris for a year. Cocktail anyone?

CHICAGO COCKTAIL

Makes 1 cocktail

2 fl oz brandy

¼ fl oz orange liqueur, such as Grand Marnier

1 dash Angostura bitters

2 fl oz Champagne or sparkling wine, chilled

Combine the brandy, orange liqueur, and bitters in a mixing glass filled with ice and stir until well chilled, 20–30 seconds. Strain into a chilled cocktail glass. Top with the Champagne or sparkling wine.

BEER NUTS

Makes 6 servings

Nonstick cooking spray, for the pan

3 cups raw peanuts

½ cup sugar

⅓ cups water

Flaky or coarse sea salt

Preheat the oven to 300°F. Line a sheet pan with aluminum foil and lightly coat with cooking spray.

In a heavy saucepan over high heat, combine the peanuts, sugar, and water and bring to a boil, stirring often. Continue to cook, stirring often, until all the liquid has evaporated and the mixture is pasty, 20–25 minutes.

Spread the peanuts in a single layer on the prepared sheet pan, breaking up any clusters, and season generously with salt. Bake, stirring once, until deep brown, 30–35 minutes. Remove from the oven, season again with salt, and serve.

French Connection

This is a riff on the classic French Connection, a blend of equal parts Cognac and amaretto. It calls for Lillet, a crisp, light French wine–based aperitif with hints of floral and citrus. Angostura and orange bitters plus a little honey simple syrup add balance and nuance to this heady mix.

makes 1 cocktail

2 fl oz Lillet

2 fl oz Cognac

2 dashes orange bitters

2 dashes Angostura bitters

½ fl oz Honey Simple Syrup (page 214)

Combine the Lillet, Cognac, bitters, and simple syrup in a shaker. Add ice, cover, shake hard for about 10 seconds, and strain into a rocks glass over ice.

Aperol Spritz

Sitting at a sidewalk café watching the world go by with a refreshing Aperol spritz is a great way to while away a late afternoon in Paris—or Milan. In episode 1, Emily wastes no time finding a café table along the Seine where she can write a few social media posts. She is soon surprised by her coworker Luc, who stops by for an amicable conversation, the start of a workplace friendship.

makes 1 cocktail

3 fl oz Prosecco, cava, or other sparkling wine

1 fl oz Aperol

Splash of club soda or seltzer

Orange slice, for garnish

Fill a highball or white-wine glass one-fourth full with ice. Add the Prosecco, Aperol, and club soda. Stir gently until mixed. Garnish with the orange slice and serve.

Sidecar

Some claim that this popular cocktail originated at the Paris Ritz in the early 1920s. Others insist it was created at the same time for a guy who arrived at Harry's New York bar in the sidecar of a motorcycle. The original recipe calls for significantly more orange liqueur. Taste the cocktail while it is still in the shaker and adjust with more liqueur (or Simple Syrup, page 214) if you prefer a sweeter drink.

makes 1 cocktail

Lemon wedge and sugar, for the rim

2 fl oz brandy

¾ fl oz orange liqueur, such as Grand Marnier

¾ fl oz fresh lemon juice

Run the lemon wedge along the rim of a chilled coupe or cocktail glass. Pour a small mound of sugar onto a flat saucer. Tip the glass so it is almost parallel to the plate and gently roll its dampened edge in the sugar to coat the rim with sugar.

Combine the brandy, orange liqueur, and lemon juice in a shaker. Add ice, cover, shake hard for about 10 seconds, and strain into the prepared glass.

Vin de Citron

Over cake and wine at La Maison Rose, Emily and Mindy express their frustration with Sylvie's demand that Emily delete her Instagram account. They decide to post "one last story" with a romp through Paris—fueled with plenty of wine. Made with lemons and white wine and fortified with eau-de-vie, this infused wine is a terrific addition to any romp. For best results use organic lemons. Serve chilled or over ice.

makes one 750-ml bottle

2 lemons

1 bottle (750 ml) dry or fruity white wine, such as Sauvignon Blanc

¾ cup eau-de-vie or vodka

½ cup sugar

½ vanilla bean, split lengthwise

Using a citrus zester, remove the zest from the lemons in long strips. Cut 1 lemon into quarters through the stem end. Reserve the other zested lemon for another use.

Combine the wine, eau-de-vie, sugar, vanilla bean, lemon zest strips, and lemon quarters in a dry, sterilized jar with a lid. Seal the jar and store in a cool, dark place for 4 days, stirring daily to dissolve the sugar.

Line a fine-mesh sieve with cheesecloth. Strain the wine through the sieve and discard the solids. Pour the wine into a dry, sterilized bottle, cover tightly, and store in a cool, dark place or in the refrigerator for up to 6 months.

French 75

At the launch party for the Fourtier flagship store, Emily reveals to Sylvie that she was able to cross-promote two of their biggest brands by dressing American actress Brooklyn Clark in Pierre Cadault, a feat certainly worthy of plenty of Champagne. This elegant Champagne cocktail—with gin, lemon, and orange bitters—would be the ideal celebratory drink, especially at a star-studded gathering in Paris.

makes 1 cocktail

1½ fl oz gin

½ fl oz fresh lemon juice

½ fl oz Simple Syrup (page 214)

3 dashes orange bitters

2 lemon zest strips

About 2 fl oz Champagne or sparkling wine, chilled

Combine the gin, lemon juice, simple syrup, bitters, and 1 zest strip in a shaker. Add ice, cover, shake hard for about 10 seconds, and strain into a chilled Champagne flute or coupe. Top with the Champagne. Express the remaining zest strip over the drink and drop it into the glass.

Boulevardier

This drink is guaranteed to keep you warm on a cold Paris night. Created in the 1920s, it was the signature drink of Erskine Gwynne, a moneyed American living in Paris who founded *The Boulevardier*, a monthly magazine. For a UK twist, choose one of the sweeter Scotch whiskies. To turn it into a Negroni, simply swap out the bourbon for gin. For a lighter cocktail, use sparkling wine in place of the bourbon.

makes 1 cocktail

1 fl oz bourbon or rye whiskey

1 fl oz sweet vermouth

1 fl oz Campari

Orange twist, for garnish

Combine the bourbon, vermouth, and Campari in a mixing glass filled with ice and stir until well chilled, 20–30 seconds. Strain into a chilled cocktail glass. Express the orange twist over the drink and drop it into the glass.

Kir Royal

What could be more romantic or more beautiful than drinking
Champagne—perhaps with a splash of crème de cassis—at a party in Paris
with the Eiffel Tower glittering in the background? At the De L'Heure
launch party, perfumer Antoine Lambert, one of Savoir's biggest clients,
flirts with Emily by spritzing her with the perfume and then seductively
describing the reasons for wearing it. *Enchantée*, Antoine.

makes 1 cocktail

5 fl oz Champagne or
sparkling wine, chilled

½ fl oz crème de cassis

Lemon twist, for garnish

Pour the Champagne and crème de cassis into a chilled champagne
flute and stir briefly. Express the lemon twist over the drink and drop
it into the glass.

Hemingway Daiquiri

Ernest Hemingway, Pablo Picasso, and other members of the literary and artistic élite put the now-famous Les Deux Magots on the map. As at the Café de Flore across the street, where Emily meets Thomas in episode 6, it is a sought-after (and touristy) rendezvous spot for sipping coffee, wine, and cocktails, such as this Havana-originated rum-based drink. Here, mint is muddled in the shaker for an added hit of fresh herbal flavor.

makes 1 cocktail

¼ cup fresh mint leaves, plus 1 sprig for garnish

2 fl oz light rum

¾ fl oz fresh lime juice

½ fl oz fresh grapefruit juice

½ fl oz maraschino liqueur

Lime slice, for garnish

In a cocktail shaker, combine the mint leaves, rum, lime juice, grapefruit juice, and maraschino liqueur and, using a cocktail muddler or a wooden spoon, gently press against the mint until it is aromatic. Fill the shaker with ice, cover, shake hard for about 10 seconds, and strain into a chilled cocktail glass. Place the mint sprig in the center of the lime slice and float on top of the drink.

Pastis Apertif

It doesn't get much simpler than this aperitif, which mixes pastis, an aniseed-flavored spirit, with water and a splash of grenadine. Ricard Pastis, traditionally simply called Ricard, was created in 1932 by Marseille-based Paul Ricard and is popular throughout France. The addition of grenadine, a deep red bar syrup, turns the drink a stunning red.

makes 1 cocktail

1 fl oz Ricard pastis

1 dash grenadine

5 fl oz ice-cold water

Fill a highball or white-wine glass one-fourth full with ice. Add the pastis and grenadine. Stir gently until mixed. Top with the water, stir again, and serve.

Vermouth Cassis Aperitif

The French make both red and white vermouth. The former is sweet, while French white (clear) vermouth is dry with subtle floral and herbal highlights. It is lovely served with just a lemon twist and sparkling water, but for a special aperitif, add a splash of crème de cassis, a dark red liqueur made from black currants that is also used in the Kir Royal on page 190.

makes 1 cocktail

3 fl oz French white vermouth

1 fl oz crème de cassis

1 fl oz fresh lemon juice

Seltzer or club soda

Lemon twist, for garnish

In a highball or collins glass, stir together the vermouth, crème de cassis, and lemon juice. Add ice cubes and top off with seltzer. Express the lemon twist over the drink and drop it into the glass.

St-Germain Fizz

Lunchtime cocktails are in order when Emily has to face Camille, Gabriel's girlfriend, fearing Camille has found out about their illicit kisses. But Camille actually invites Emily to her family's château to pitch Savoir to Maman. This light-as-a-breeze drink, made with St-Germain (elderflower liqueur), gin, lemon juice, and sparkling wine, is ideal midday—or any time of day.

makes 1 cocktail

1½ fl oz gin

1 fl oz St-Germain

1 fl oz lemon juice

3 fl oz Champagne or sparkling wine. chilled

Lemon twist. for garnish

Combine the gin, St-Germain, and lemon juice in a shaker. Add ice, cover, shake hard for about 10 seconds, and strain into a chilled champagne flute. Top with the Champagne. Express the lemon twist over the drink and drop it into the glass.

French Rose

This pretty cocktail is a blushing pink—perhaps the color of Emily's face after she and Gabriel kiss for the time? A simple concoction of gin, dry vermouth, and cherry brandy, it's a gorgeous drink to share with a lover in Paris—or anywhere.

makes 1 cocktail

3 fl oz gin

1 fl oz dry French vermouth

1 fl oz cherry brandy

Combine the gin, vermouth, and brandy in a shaker. Add ice, cover, shake hard for about 10 seconds, and strain into a chilled coupe or cocktail glass.

Mimosa

This cocktail of Champagne and orange juice is a great choice when celebrating with friends. That's especially true if the friends are visiting from China to watch their best friend, Mindy, belt out a song—immediately redeeming herself after an embarrassing appearance on *Chinese Popstar*. Make sure to have an extra bottle of Champagne on hand to spray the cheering crowd. One bottle to drink and one bottle—Champère—to spray is how Emily pitches it to Camille's mother, Louise.

makes 1 cocktail

2 fl oz fresh orange juice, chilled

4 fl oz Champagne or
sparkling wine, chilled

Pour the orange juice into a champagne flute, then top with the Champagne.

Tequila Sunrise Shots

Brooklyn Clark surprises Emily by running out of the Fourtier launch party wearing a $2 million watch for which Emily is responsible, ending up in a loud nightclub. It's no wonder that Emily agrees to "just 'one' fun drink." A tequila shot seems to be Brooklyn's favorite party drink, and this version, dressed up with orange juice, grenadine, and a salted rim is just the ticket to get a party pumping.

makes 6 shots

Salt for rimming glass

1 lime wedge

8 fl oz fresh orange juice

4 fl oz tequila

1 fl oz grenadine

On a small plate, spread an even layer of salt. Gently rub the lime wedge around the rim of six 2-oz shot glasses. Holding the base of the glass, dip the rims in the salt. Set the glasses aside.

Fill a cocktail shaker half full with ice and add the orange juice and tequila. Cover, shake hard for about 20 seconds, and strain into the shot glasses, dividing it evenly. Top each shot with a little of the grenadine, slowly pouring it over the back of a spoon into the glass.

Corpse Reviver

For eighty-five years, beginning in 1914, absinthe—known as the "green fairy"—was banned in France because it was mistakenly believed to have mind-altering properties. This cocktail, made from absinthe, gin, orange liqueur, and Cocchi Americano (mildly bitter aperitif wine), won't alter anything except your mood—for the better. It is also reputed to cure a hangover, thus its name.

makes 1 cocktail

1 fl oz gin

1 fl oz Cocchi Americano

1 fl oz orange liqueur, such as Grand Marnier

1 fl oz fresh lemon juice

2 dashes absinthe

Combine gin, Cocchi Americano, orange liqueur, lemon juice, and absinthe in a shaker. Add ice, cover, shake hard for about 10 seconds, and strain into a chilled coupe or cocktail glass.

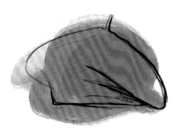

SIX
LES BASES

Mignonette Sauce

makes about ¾ cup

⅔ cup champagne or rice vinegar

2 tablespoons fresh lemon juice

2 tablespoons minced shallot

Fine sea salt and freshly
ground black pepper

In a small serving bowl, stir together the vinegar, lemon juice, and shallot. Season with salt and pepper. Cover and refrigerate until serving.

Crostini

makes 25 toasts

25 baguette slices, each
about ¼ inch thick

Olive oil, for brushing

Fine sea salt and freshly
ground black pepper

Preheat the oven to 375°F. Lightly brush the bread slices on both sides with oil, then season lightly on both sides with salt and pepper. Arrange on a sheet pan. Bake until just golden, 10–12 minutes. Transfer to a platter or tray and let cool. (The crostini can be prepared up to 1 hour in advance and set aside, or they can be prepared a day in advance and stored in an airtight container at room temperature overnight.)

Pomme Frites

makes 2 servings

4 russet potatoes, about
2 lb total weight

Canola oil, for deep-frying

Kosher salt

Peel the potatoes and cut lengthwise into slices about ¼ inch thick. Then cut the slices lengthwise into strips about ¼ inch thick. Transfer the potato strips to a bowl of cold water and let stand for about 15 minutes to remove excess starch.

Pour the oil to a depth of 2 inches into a large, heavy pot and heat the oil over high heat to 330°F on a deep-frying thermometer. Have ready a pair of long tongs or a large wire skimmer. Line a sheet pan with paper towels and set it next to the stove top.

While the oil heats, drain the potatoes and dry them well with kitchen towels. (Wet potatoes will stick together and cause the oil to splatter.) Working in batches, carefully add 3 large handfuls of the potatoes to the pot. The oil will expand and should cover them. Fry until the potatoes are lightly golden but have not started to brown, 4–5 minutes. Using the tongs or skimmer, transfer the potatoes to the prepared sheet pan to drain. Repeat with the remaining potatoes in batches, always letting the oil return to 330°F and scooping out any potato bits before adding the next batch. Reserve the oil in the pan off the heat. The partially fried potatoes will keep at room temperature for up to 2 hours.

Reheat the oil for the fries to 370°F. Line a large sheet pan with paper towels and set it next to the stove top. Working in the same-size batches, add the potatoes to the hot oil and fry until golden brown and crisp, 3–5 minutes. Transfer to the fresh paper towels. When all the potatoes are fried, transfer them to a plate or shallow serving bowl and season generously with salt.

Croissant Dough

makes 2 lb dough

1 envelope (2¼ teaspoons) active dry yeast

2 tablespoons sugar

3 tablespoons lukewarm water (105°–115°F)

1 teaspoon fine sea salt

1 cup cold unsalted butter, plus 2 tablespoons, melted and cooled

1 cup cold whole milk

2½ cups plus 2 tablespoons all-purpose flour

In a small bowl, stir the yeast and 1 tablespoon of the sugar into the warm water until the yeast dissolves. Let stand until foamy, about 10 minutes.

In a large bowl, combine the remaining 1 tablespoon sugar, the salt, the 2 tablespoons melted butter, the milk, and ½ cup of the flour. Add the yeast mixture and stir with a wooden spoon until blended. Gradually add 2 cups of the flour, mixing just until the dough comes together in a sticky mass. (Alternatively, mix the dough on medium speed in a stand mixer fitted with the paddle attachment.)

Line a sheet pan with parchment paper. On a lightly floured work surface, roll out the dough into a rectangle about ½ inch thick. Transfer the dough to the prepared sheet pan, cover with plastic wrap, and refrigerate until chilled, about 40 minutes.

Using a rolling pin or the heel of your hand, knead or beat the 1 cup butter on a work surface to flatten it and warm it to about 60°F (checked with an instant-read thermometer). Sprinkle the butter with the remaining 2 tablespoons flour and gently beat the butter with the rolling pin to press the flour into it. Shape the butter into a 6×8-inch rectangle. If the butter has become too warm, wrap and refrigerate just until firm but still pliable (60°F).

On a lightly floured work surface, roll out the dough into a 9×13-inch rectangle. Place the chilled butter on the lower half of the dough, leaving a ½-inch border on all sides. Fold over the upper half of the dough to cover the butter and press the edges together to seal. With the folded side to your left, roll out the dough into a 10×24-inch rectangle. With a short side facing you, fold the bottom third up and then fold the top third down, as if folding a letter. This completes the first turn. Wrap the dough in plastic wrap, place on a sheet pan, and refrigerate for 45 minutes.

Return the chilled dough to a lightly floured work surface with a folded side to your left and repeat the process, rolling the dough into a 10×24-inch rectangle and folding it into thirds like a letter. Wrap in plastic wrap and chill for 45 minutes. Repeat twice for two more turns, for a total of four turns. After the final turn, refrigerate the dough for at least 4 hours or up to overnight. (At this point, you can also freeze the dough for longer storage. Wrap tightly with plastic wrap, slip into a lock-top plastic freezer bag, and freeze for up to 1 month, then thaw in the refrigerator before continuing.)

Tarte Dough

makes enough dough for 1 tart

1 large egg yolk

1 teaspoon pure vanilla extract

2 tablespoons very cold water

1¼ cups all-purpose flour

3 tablespoons sugar

¼ teaspoon fine sea salt

½ cup cold unsalted butter, cut into small pieces

In a small bowl, stir together the egg yolk, vanilla, and water. In a food processor, combine the flour, sugar, and salt and pulse two or three times to mix. Scatter the butter over the flour mixture and pulse for a few seconds, just until the butter is broken up into the flour. Pour the egg mixture over the flour mixture, then process just until the dough starts to come together. Dump the dough into a large lock-top plastic bag, press into a flat disk, and seal closed. Refrigerate for at least 30 minutes or up to 1 day before using. (Or freeze for up to 1 month, then thaw in the refrigerator before using.)

Pastry Cream

makes about 2 cups

1½ cups whole milk

4 large egg yolks

⅓ cup granulated sugar

3 tablespoons cornstarch

⅛ teaspoon fine sea salt

1½ teaspoons pure vanilla extract

Pour the milk into a saucepan and heat over medium heat until small bubbles appear along the pan edge and steam begins to rise from the milk. Remove from the heat. In a bowl, whisk together the egg yolks and granulated sugar until pale yellow. Whisk in the cornstarch and salt until dissolved. Gradually pour half of the hot milk into the yolk mixture while whisking constantly. Whisk in the remaining milk and then pour the combined mixture into the saucepan. Cook over medium-low heat, whisking constantly, until the mixture thickens to a pudding-like consistency, 5–6 minutes. Do not let it boil. Scrape into a bowl and whisk in the vanilla. Cover the bowl with plastic wrap, pressing it directly onto the surface of the pastry cream. Refrigerate until chilled, 2–3 hours.

White Chocolate Buttercream

makes about 2 cups

2 oz white chocolate, finely chopped

4 tablespoons unsalted butter, at room temperature

1¼ cups confectioners' sugar

1½ tablespoons whole milk

1 teaspoon pure vanilla extract

Pinch of fine sea salt

Put the chocolate into a heatproof bowl and set over (not touching) barely simmering water in a saucepan. Heat, stirring often, until the chocolate melts and is smooth. Let cool for about 10 minutes.

In another bowl, using an electric mixer on medium speed, beat the butter until light and fluffy, about 2 minutes. Stop the mixer and scrape down the bowl sides with a rubber spatula. On medium speed, beat in the sugar, milk, vanilla, and salt until well mixed, then add the white chocolate and beat until blended. Stop the mixer and scrape down the bowl sides. Then beat on medium-high speed until the frosting is fluffy and smooth, about 5 minutes. Use right away, or store in an airtight container in the refrigerator for up to 2 days. Stir vigorously just before using.

Simple Syrup

makes about 1½ cups

1 cup water

1 cup sugar

In a small saucepan over medium-high heat, bring the water to a simmer. Add the sugar and stir until the sugar is dissolved. Remove from the heat and let cool. Strain the syrup through a fine-mesh sieve into a clean container, cover, and refrigerate for up to one month.

Honey Simple Syrup To make honey simple syrup, omit the sugar and combine equal parts honey and water over medium heat, stirring until the honey dissolves, then let cool.

Caramel Syrup

makes about ½ cup

⅔ cup sugar

1 tablespoon water

In a heavy saucepan over medium heat, combine the sugar and water. Cook, stirring with a wooden spoon, until the sugar dissolves. Continue to cook without stirring until a light caramel syrup forms, 4–8 minutes. Remove from the heat and use right away, or store in an airtight container in the refrigerator for up to 2 months.

Table of Equivalents

The exact equivalents in the following tables have been rounded for convenience.

Liquid and Dry Measurements

U.S.	METRIC
¼ teaspoon	1.25 milliliters
½ teaspoon	2.5 milliliters
1 teaspoon	5 milliliters
1 tablespoon (3 teaspoons)	15 milliliters
1 fluid ounce	30 milliliters
¼ cup	65 milliliters
⅓ cup	80 milliliters
1 cup	235 milliliters
1 pint (2 cups)	480 milliliters
1 quart (4 cups, 32 fluid ounces)	950 milliliters
1 gallon (4 quarts)	3.8 liters
1 ounce (by weight)	28 grams
1 pound	454 grams
2.2 pounds	1 kilogram

Length Measures

U.S.	METRIC
⅛ inch	3 millimeters
¼ inch	6 millimeters
½ inch	12 millimeters
1 inch	2.5 centimeters

Oven Temperatures

FAHRENHEIT	CELSIUS	GAS
250°	120°	½
275°	140°	1
300°	150°	2
325°	160°	3
350°	180°	4
375°	190°	5
400°	200°	6
425°	220°	7
450°	230°	8
475°	240°	9
500°	260°	10

Index

weldon**owen**

PO Box 3088
San Rafael, CA 94912
www.weldonowen.com

WELDON OWEN INTERNATIONAL
CEO Raoul Goff
Publisher Roger Shaw
Associate Publisher Amy Marr
Editorial Director Katie Killebrew
Assistant Editor Jourdan Plautz
VP of Creative Chrissy Kwasnik
Design Support Amy DeGrote
Production Manager Joshua Smith
Sr Production Manager, Subsidiary Rights Lina s Palma-Temena

Project Editor Kim Laidlaw
Photography Waterbury Publications, Des Moines, IA
Food Stylist Jennifer Peterson

A WELDON OWEN PRODUCTION

Printed and bound in China

All rights reserved. No part of this book may be reproduced in any form without written permission from the publisher.

First printed in 2022
10 9 8 7 6 5 4 3 2 1

Library of Congress Cataloging in Publication data is available

ISBN: 978-1-68188-881-1

Weldon Owen would also like to thank Sharon Silva.